I0529961

MASTERING MIND MUD IN SCHOOLS

ELEVATE MINDSETS, GRADUATE WINNERS

MASTERING MIND MUD IN SCHOOLS

ELEVATE MINDSETS, GRADUATE WINNERS

NEIL FESER

Niche Pressworks
Indianapolis, IN

MASTERING MIND MUD IN SCHOOLS: Elevate Mindsets, Graduate Winners
Copyright © 2025 by Neil Feser

All rights reserved. No part of this book may be used or reproduced in any manner whatsoever without prior written consent of the author, except as provided by the United States of America copyright law.

No part of this book or any work of Neil Feser, including *Insight Presentations*, *Skills Through Presentations*, or downloads from any of Neil Feser's works, including neilfeser.com, masteringmindmud.com, or associated websites, may be entered into any version of AI, artificial intelligence, to create or develop another version.

For permission to reprint portions of this content or bulk purchases, contact neilfeser@neilfeser.com.

No claim to prevent any or all suicides is made, intended, or implied through the use of the material or advice given in this book, Mastering Mind Mud LLC, presentations or speeches by Neil Feser, his employees, and associates; or the content and advice in the *Skills Through Presentation* program in any and all formats.

Author photos by Melanie Langteau of Milestone Photography

Published by Niche Pressworks; NichePressworks.com
Indianapolis, IN

ISBN
Hardcover: 978-1-962956-59-8
Paperback: 978-1-962956-58-1
eBook: 978-1-962956-60-4

Library of Congress Cataloging-in-Publication Data on File at lccn.loc.gov.

The views expressed herein are solely those of the author and do not necessarily reflect the views of the publisher.

*Thank you, Grayce, for your extraordinary life
of building great mindsets in the people you touched.*

ACKNOWLEDGEMENTS

Many students, parents, and educators deserve thanks for challenging me to create and offer means to assist them.

Thanks to Johynne Gerhardt and Lori Wildhagen for their contributions and insights in the development of the *Skills Through Presentations* program. Students grow because of you.

A special thank you to everyone working with Niche Pressworks for their professionalism and care.

TABLE OF CONTENTS

WINNING HEARTS AND MINDS

To teach children, you must enter their view of the world!

Working with teachers across the country for the last 20 years has reinforced my belief that if we win the hearts of students, their minds will follow. Kids are and always will be more important than any material we are trying to teach them.

Mastering Mind Mud in Schools offers a unique cognitive approach. It teaches educators how to address the heart issues that affect students, especially those that cloud their minds.

Neil Feser's techniques and tricks give educators a way to fill up a child's gas tank before the accelerator is pushed. When teachers make kids feel seen, heard, and validated in the classroom, teaching any concept is *so* much easier, and Feser shows every teacher how to do just that!

Neil's gift is cleaning up troubles through presentations with relatable visual hooks. Once, when observing Neil address a gym full of high schoolers, I overheard a kid say, "I never know what he is going to do, but I know it will be about me."

Feser's *Skills Through Presentations* program shows educators how to visually catch students' attention and keep it! For kids to effectively process academic content, they must see it, hear it, feel it, do it, relate it to something they already know, and explain it to somebody else. To do this effectively, the "Mind Mud" must be cleared away first. When this fails to happen, cognitive understanding and emotional regulation compete for brain attention making learning much more difficult.

We can never have too many great ideas out there when it comes to teaching kids. Thank you, Neil Feser, for sharing your gifts!

Welcome into the creative mind of one of the best educators I have ever met!

— JULIA COOK

INTRODUCTION

IMPROVE THE FLOW OF SUCCESS

You will get all you want in life if you help
enough other people get what they want.
— ZIG ZIGLAR

For decades, as a counselor, teacher, author, and professional presenter, I have worked to walk the talk. These pages are based much more on experience than theory to help students excel, graduate from high school, go on to higher education, and become leaders in their families, fields, and communities. I have paid my dues. My goal with *Mastering Mind Mud* is to help you to walk the walk faster and more efficiently so that you pay fewer dues. We need mud-free mindsets that move.

My mission statement is: To improve the flow of success — for students, parents, educators, and society.

My goal is to help transition your mindset upward to be and do more. I will show you where you can access my broader work, publications, and resources to assist you in elevating student mindsets and skills to make their successes inevitable. Everyone grows. Success flows.

Early in my professional writing career, I wrote comedy. Extra words do not fly in comedy. This trained me to save you reading time. We have things to do. Let's act. Let's go.

CHAPTER 1

DO NOT GO OUT THERE — RUN OUT

Think like a man of action;
act like a man of thought.
— HENRI BERGSON

"If something happens in the hall, you don't go out there." Others nodded in agreement with the student who spoke to me, a slender, student teacher who looked young enough to be sitting with them instead of standing at the front of the room. The members of this speech class at the inner-city Technical High School in Omaha, Nebraska, must have liked me.

They could have said, "If something happens in the hall, it really helps if you go out there."

1

In that moment a question formed. How can I get involved to make a difference in student lives — one that helps them focus on their education despite the challenges they face?

At my next school, Cathedral High School, twenty blocks away from Tech High, a student felt cornered and acted out. This time, I was in the hallway and saw him pull a knife. He had transferred from a school where that move must have worked to get others to back down, but he'd forgotten that he didn't need a knife at this school. I saw in his eyes that he was just scared. Knowing the students around him better than he did, I was able to diffuse the situation.

Again, I wondered how I could create a positive impact in his life so that outside struggles would not negatively affect his ability to focus on his studies and prevent him from achieving future success.

I knew there was a way.

WARNING AND INDICTMENT

"You don't go out there" was both a warning and an indictment. Is it the job of educators to address non-content issues, or is it an opportunity? How can educators best address issues outside classrooms that are captivating the minds in the classrooms? Teachers affect what goes on in the larger "Life Hallways" by effectively and creatively addressing them inside classrooms through a multi-level, textured, teamwork approach. Stress, worry, and what I call "muddy thinking" are not in the usual teacher's lesson plan, but they affect the success of lessons if not addressed. Fortunately, it is possible to address muddy thinking in targeted lesson plans.

Teaching becomes more effective when student minds are on the subject, not their problems. Attracting minds to the classroom and subject matter is not the responsibility of one teacher. This should be a multi-level, multi-room effort championed by a group of teachers who work in a coordinated effort to change student perceptions and help them uplift life skills. Many students will see a teacher's effort and figure out that the staff cares for them as people. As a result, they trust the teachers more, and they behave better too.

Education and life are not complicated if people know what buttons to push. The job of educators is to push their best buttons to better help students find and push their own. So, how do we simplify what seems complicated?

Complicated things are best approached and conveyed as flows of simplicity. Simple things do not scare people away. When properly arranged, sequences of simplicity evolve into sophisticated, understood, and accepted practices and procedures. With practice, the former complex problem is now approached with confidence by people who know they are prepared with great choices, paths, solutions, or options. This concept is expanded in coming chapters.

> Complicated things are best approached and conveyed as flows of simplicity.

Educators control the narrative in schools, while social media and their surroundings influence how students grow. At times, it seems like a battle where students are caught in the middle, seeking their own narrative. Many things in their lives "muddy up" or make their thinking unclear, such as fears, misinformation, worries, poor self-images, and doubts.

Muddy thinking is not limited to students. Educators and parents or guardians (hereafter referred to as parents) experience muddy thinking too. In truth, everyone experiences similar things, even if at more sophisticated levels. All humans are challenged to get their thoughts out of the mud or the mud out of their thoughts. We know everyone functions better when clearheaded. It is something we can teach by using clear, easy-to-understand exercises.

Educators can help clear up muddy thinking by addressing what their experience shows that students need. Students often see part of what educators do but may lack the self-discipline to act on their own. We can build on that. Students bring the kindling. Educators bring the wood.

From the student perspective, education must be relevant or at least mildly interesting. Older people like to blame modern life for a lack of self-discipline, but if we're honest, we can admit it was basically the same for us. For the "ancients," a radio was a distraction. Now, "radios" are everywhere.

What are the messages on those current radios? Where are the young being led? What Hallways are they being led down? Who is leading them? Do they have the skills and clear thinking to follow the right leads? Positioning students' minds to have the skills and emotional strength needed is an opportunity for educators to step up so their students — the future of the community — are not led astray.

At times, we are all afraid to venture out into our Life Hallway. The unknown can be scary. It also can be safe and great. Everyone has been in a big school, hospital, or building and taken the wrong hallway. There may be nothing wrong with that hallway. It is just not the right one for us. It is easy to ask for help, but will students "go out there" and ask for help to reach their best futures? Many will not if educators do not light the way, then lead, and, at times, herd them forward.

Students often talk big and know or demonstrate little. It shows in subject matter and, at times, in other areas that also matter. Here, the reference is to enhance the development of Core Values+ like honesty and respect. I use the term Core Values+ as a generic term to include growth techniques, acquired skill sets, etc. Those are common-sense issues and concepts teachers value and should be willing to communicate along with subject matter. Educators should not think of Core Values+ as unknowns because they model them daily. Beyond modeling them, teaching them can be great and expand a teacher's repertoire. Later, we will get into how this effort enhances and makes relevant the delivery of content.

How does this help a teacher in the classroom? Who would a teacher rather teach? A room full of orderly, respectful, engaged students? Or a group of loudmouths with little respect? The same answer is true in all rooms of the building. Educators are in this together.

How do we get those Core Values+ across? Initially, it takes effort, but once in the curriculum, it becomes repetition and an expectation of both students and educators. Which does a teacher want to spend time on? Preventing problems before they happen? Or repeatedly fixing them in the hallways?

Infusing Core Values+ fixes many problems and eliminates students' muddy thinking, conferences, calls to parents, arguments, detentions, and paperwork. If students respect each other, there is much less bullying, antagonizing others, or mud-throwing. Life is not hard if we act to make it easier. No one wants the alternative.

I began as an idealist. Idealists know how to fix the world. All the world must do is listen to them. Successive years of experience taught me that fixing the world is a little more complicated than that. Ironically, to get anywhere, it may be necessary to be a little naïve. Fully understanding how tough it may be to make significant changes can dampen the enthusiasm required to start change. Students may get stuck, but educators are not allowed to live stuck in mental or action mud, no matter how deep or challenging the mud is. To educate is to significantly change the trajectory of student lives — their whole lives, not only their GPAs.

A fire of idealism must be refocused into the fire of action to solve real problems and challenges. We will deepen this in Chapter 9. Acting produces more results than only knowing. Idealistically, educators present material students gleefully absorb. Except, life happens and intercedes.

In a room of 25 students, non-curriculum content issues like bullying, lack of confidence, drug use, laziness, low interest in the subject, or general worries may be dominating many student's thoughts. Half of those students may really care but are misfocused. By reducing distracting thoughts in the room, teaching suddenly improves. Almighty test scores may even go up. Integrated improvements elevate the school. Even single-digit improvements in many areas of the school have synergy and elevate those around them.

Many youths live in distractions and assume life will work for them because it is just supposed to happen. They choose to coast instead of putting in a reasonable amount of work to make their futures feel like coasting, not the harsher reality of lower-paying jobs early coasting earns.

I had advantages. I liked to learn, and my parents made sure I did not coast. It may take the intercession of others to propel us into our future. At times, intercession is a teacher. It was for me. Why did I decide to teach speech before becoming a counselor, and how did that decision lead to multiple successes? How did the encouragement and opportunities offered by my high school speech teacher affect my future? How did the warning given to me by the students at Tech High School transition into multiple approaches to address student growth and help prevent an indictment of many futures? Read on.

IT STARTED WITH FIRE AND BRIMSTONE

The first time I spoke in my high school speech class was a colorful experience. My face and neck turned red. Humbled, I survived. We almost always survive. We thrive if we learn from loss and apply the lessons. That is an important lesson to know and keep close when trying anything new and a great lesson to model and present to students. Prior to prosperity, everyone must take their lumps. I had to find a horse to get back up on. With perfect timing, it came my way.

Mrs. Thummel, my speech teacher, assigned a harangue, an exaggerated, over-the-top speech designed to stretch us out of our comfort and discomfort zones. She wanted over-the-top, so I went for it with the speech, *Reverend Wickens Rids the World of Its Wild, Wicked, and Wretched Ways.* He was the idealist who demanded that others act.

My fire and brimstone preacher's delivery led Mrs. Thummel to ask my accounting teacher to release me from his class so I could perform it for another of her speech classes. She then asked me to perform it at my first speech contest, — the District Speech Tournament — which was the last one of the year. Winning it sent me to the State Speech Tournament. At District, one judge was happy with what I did. The other judge thought I should tone it down. I made the mistake of trying to please both. My middle-of-the-road presentation at State was not the same. I learned. Never throw half a fastball, half a compliment, half a program, or half of the truth. Commit to being successful.

The early speech work led to a college major in speech and to improvisational acting with *Sweetness and Light* in Omaha's Old Market district. These foreshadowed my work designing visually impactful presentations to effectively address life and death problems like suicide and drug use, dealing with stress and bullying, and uplifting students by addressing leadership and other opportunities. Would it have happened without a nudge from my teacher?

So, how can this help you, the reader? A big fear of educators is the

> Never throw half a fastball, half a compliment, half a program, or half of the truth. Commit to being successful.

loss of students to suicide. It can tear up a school. In Chapter 6, you will be introduced to the free, downloadable presentation *Bad Year, Great Life.* Its powerful visual impact makes it effective. In my career, I never lost a student to suicide and attribute that to taking preventative action.

In Chapter 6, you will also see how presentations like *Dropouts Drop Dollars* serve multiple purposes by reducing dropouts and the commission of financial suicide. Because they stay in school, the saved students benefit from the additional academic and life lessons educators will present in their junior and senior years.

Success follows, clearing up short-sighted, muddy thinking and acquiring the proper growth mindset. No lecture is required when the message is clear. Visual images and math do the talking.

MAKE YOUR WORLD, OR IT WILL MAKE YOU

A sorrowful yet valuable lesson from that Tech High School speech class when I was a young teacher helped set the course for my professional life as a counselor and presenter. Easily the best speaker in my class was a regal young woman named Delilah, who spoke with poise and confidence. She always gave an impressive performance through her bearing and skill. Then, Delilah went out into her Hallway — her real life.

Years passed, and I became a poor graduate student without a washer and dryer. One day, I walked through the door of a local laundromat and into her Hallway. The real world hit me in the face. Delilah, the best, most skilled speaker from my Tech High speech class, was the laundro-mat attendant. There is nothing wrong with honest work, but I wondered what happened to such enormous potential.

Where was the proper guidance she deserved? Why did we lose what her talent could offer our world? What intercepted a better career for this young woman? Why was she not a teacher, sales representative, young executive, banker, or in public relations? Was she made aware of such opportunities so she could choose the best paths for her future? Did she not have a choice to pursue additional education and, instead, had to go to work? Did no one help her find ways to make both immediate and future earning options work? Did her counselor not get out of the office to serve the hallways?

And why didn't the young, shocked, idealistic me not do what I would do now — find out what went wrong and offer to show her ways to renew and rebuild? I probably thought it was not my place. If I'd known what I know now, I would have assigned each member of that speech class to give a speech on some aspect of careers or finishing and furthering their education. Yes, that is a suggestion for your communications program.

Speech and communication courses are designed to improve speech and delivery skills, but career-focused content will do more than get students learning about hobbies or random topics. When students talk, other students listen more than when the teacher does. Use this to help your counselors help more students upgrade their goals. The counseling department has the resources and information. Invite a counselor into your classroom to watch some speeches and add post-speech comments. You will get great results.

Maybe Delilah is making her mark now. She made her mark on me. I do not want to look back and think about a young person I did not help when I had a chance. Maybe she is making her biggest mark through my work and how it has helped others who will, in turn, help more. Thank you, Delilah!

When counselors serve hundreds of students each year, it is impossible to help them all in every way they need. Educators work hard to help as many as they can. It is what educators do. Pervasive development in a school requires a systematic approach, not the great, but random actions of isolated teachers. I applaud those, but their efforts are not enough to get everyone on the same positive page. We make our world, or it makes us. We make our schools, or outside influences make it difficult.

Little things can be important in shaping students' futures and multiplying successes. The observations and occurrences in my educational background show that minor experiences in the big world are often major for those we help. As educators create multi-level opportunities for young people to see and attain better futures, they move closer to the greatness they deserve. Is this book about elevating the mindsets of students or of educators? Both. It is the synergy inherent in the great teaching of learning and learning great teaching.

When an educator displays excellence, the more important lesson may be in a hidden life-growth message folded into an academic content presentation. The student picks it up without being told, draws their conclusion, which they are more willing to accept, and incorporates it into their thinking and life. It is subtle teaching. It is building worlds.

It is fine to only teach the subject matter, but is that game on? Great teaching requires subtle, diligent, creative work to help students acquire the skills they may not know they need until they are attracted to those conclusions and find the vision and mindsets to see, develop, and own skills on their own. Great teachers are world-builders.

> Great teaching requires subtle, diligent, creative work to help students acquire the skills they may not know they need until they are attracted to those conclusions and find the vision and mindsets to see, develop, and own skills on their own. Great teachers are world-builders.

YOU WON'T DRINK IT, SO DON'T THINK IT

The traditional half-full or half-empty glass of water is less inviting if the water is muddy. We all have times when it is hard for us to get through muddy thinking. Doubt, fear, illogic, lies, misinformation, etc., muddy our thoughts. The goal is to reduce, manage, or master muddy thinking in as many areas as possible.

The title of this book is *Mastering Mind Mud in Schools*, so I'd argue the goal is mastery, but realistically, that is a tall order. We know mastery is impossible because every year, we get a new grade level of students and transfers to initiate into the program, yet we cannot shoot for 83.7 percent mastery and leave out a significant group of students. We must strive to elevate all and reach as many as we can. Again, the title is *Mastering*, not *Mastered Mind Mud in Schools*.

Do not think you cannot reach all of them, even if that mud exists. Instead, believe you can lead them all to the fountain to drink. It might take a year or two, but eventually, most will get thirsty. Stay in the fight. The world will never stop fighting back. You are not alone. We are fighting together.

It is not hard to wash our hair. That is an activity. People do not worry much while washing their hair. In a sense, we should wash our thoughts too. Getting active often easily gets the mind off problems because the activity requires attention. Simple solutions often slay complex problems. In the following box is a way of understanding the cumulative effects of muddy thoughts.

TOILET PAPER BONDS

In one of my presentations, a volunteer puts their palms together, and I wrap toilet paper twice around the joined hands. Each wrap represents a muddy, hindering thought. The volunteer can easily separate the hands as they can their mind from a couple of muddy thoughts. After rejoining the hands, I wrap the toilet paper around them again and say each wrap represents a negative thought. After many wraps, they feel the restrictiveness of excessive muddy thinking.

Flipping the perspective, what if all the wraps, the thoughts, are positive and meant to hold the person's act together and promote growth? Everyone gets it.

More presentation examples and *Skills Through Presentations* information will be found in boxes like this. If interested, read them. If not, simply skip.

THE ROAD TO EXCELLENCE GOES THROUGH BASICS

We do not need to separate Core Values+ and educational subject matters. It is often possible to integrate and convey both at the same time. While focusing on one, people are elevated by the other. Often, they are interested and able to see the bigger picture, where life skills fit, and where subject matter fits. A life of excellence is a combination of basic but intriguing blends.

Education is not complicated. Identify important things, then find the most interesting and effective ways to convey them. Experience, research, and inspiration are coupled with the courage to find and use what really works. If a teaching strategy, tactic, or attempt to do something new does not work, so what? Learn to laugh about it. If students see their teacher taking screw-ups lightly when trying something new, they relax and are willing to try new things too. It is safe to attempt to learn tough things in math, language, and science.

Forward movement is possible, but accelerating progress is seldom made by doing something the same way. If a teacher is still using the same lesson plans from five years ago, they are more concerned with being safe than being better. They are not exemplifying learning.

Life becomes complicated by stress, lack of time and money, worry, and negative

> Education is not complicated. Identify important things, then find the most interesting and effective ways to convey them. Experience, research, and inspiration are coupled with the courage to find and use what really works.

influences and obstacles in families and communities. Thinking gets muddy when minds stop focusing on the most important opportunities.

Am I talking about the focus of students or educators? Both, of course. See each student as an opportunity, challenge, and an awakening of teaching skills.

Sports are great teachers. In sports, the physical Core Values+, the basics of footwork, positioning, etc., are incredibly important. A great athlete with poor footwork can still beat an average athlete with great footwork. But if two great athletes meet and only one has great footwork, that skilled athlete will defeat the one with poorer foot skills. Not sometimes — every time.

To gain excellence, we must believe in, support, and promote educational and behavioral basics. That is our mindset. If students cannot read, write, do math, and communicate well, they will not get far in their careers and lives. None of that is hard. Teaching the skills is not hard. Instead, getting students to believe in the need for the skill is often the challenge. Why? Because not trying, social media distractions, laziness, and muddy thinking about potential personal futures are easier. We will target how to address and draw in the students in later chapters.

In my youth, I learned that water flows along the path of least resistance. Water does not seek a hose or pipe. It does not go looking for a faucet. It is pretty as it flows down a stream, but it will not stop and say hello or give us a drink. We must guide the flow.

Guiding water is easy when compared to guiding student energy. Many students are self-starters, but modern student energy can seek too many paths of least resistance. We must help the self-starters a little, the partial starters a lot, and the non-starters much more to prevent them from becoming failures who only pursue the paths of least resistance.

In school, it was always easier for me to work with a student who caused problems than one who sat like a rock doing nothing. Eventually, and often with help, a problem student would redirect their energy and move onto a better path.

It is harder, but not impossible, to motivate a rock. That is why we must start early and not let rock-like habits set in. Once that mindset is there and the student figures out how to get by without really working, the road is longer and steeper. In these cases, it is best to use a multi-level strategy. Teach one thing and let the subtext carry the message the rock needs to learn.

At lunch duty or in a hallway, I might walk up to a table or group and tell one student something that was fitting for them, but it was really intended for someone else close by who really needed to hear it. Similarly, teachers may make a statement to the entire class or group that is only intended for one student. The student needs to get the message without being singled out or lectured because that is all they ever thought they heard and turned off. Subterfuge can be great.

Part of an educator's job is to direct student energy to places that help them grow in ways not imagined. Once the habit of seeking challenging sources and resources takes over, we must get out of the way and have faith that the values we've helped foster kick in so the results are productive and valuable.

If people learn and practice respect, caring, giving everyone space, telling the truth — Core Values+ — most potential interaction problems will take care of themselves.

A recurring theme asks, "Are we executing the basics?" If we are, we will frame or set up students for success. If we are not, it is just a matter of time before the educational train goes off the track.

Educators are in control of the environment in schools, but students, as do all of us, remain in control of what they want and allow into their heads. Educators must address how to best attract students to the best behaviors and thinking for their futures. Fortunately, there are ways for educators to raise their games so students can raise theirs.

Most educators want to grow. All must be supplied with the best means to do so. Fortunately, the means are within reach. As will be later referenced in terms of coaching, achieving excellence follows executing the simplicity of basics, which then evolve into the sophisticated. Keep it simple. Keep it going. Absorb this to develop and share an aspiring mindset. Sophistication awaits. You are going to be so good!

> If people learn and practice respect, caring, giving everyone space, telling the truth — Core Values+ — most potential interaction problems will take care of themselves.

THINGS TO REMEMBER AND APPLY

○ Teachers are likely to find their teaching more effective when students' minds are on the subject, not on personal problems. Redirecting minds should be a multi-level, multi-room approach that improves academic and social-emotional development.

○ All humans are challenged to get their thoughts out of the mud or the mud out of their thoughts.

○ Infusing Core Values+ fixes many problems and eliminates students' muddy thinking, conferences, calls to parents, detentions, etc. Success follows cleaning up short-sighted, muddy thinking and acquiring a growth mindset. Clear messages eliminate lectures.

○ Pervasive development in a school requires a systematic approach. We make our school environments or outside influencers make them difficult.

○ Synergy reverberates in great teaching and learning to teach great. There is also synergy uniting Core Values+ and educational subject matters. It is often possible to integrate and convey both at the same time. While focusing on one, people are elevated by the other.

○ To gain excellence, we must believe in, support, and promote educational and behavioral basics, the base of great mindsets.

CHAPTER 2

SUCCESSFUL LEADERS STAND UP TO PROBLEMS

You've got to think about the "big things" while you're doing the small things, so that all the small things go in the right direction.
— ALVIN TOFFLER

Note: This chapter is aimed at administrators and counselors, but others can learn from added perspectives because everyone in a school is a leader of young people and each other. Big things are eventually executed through doing the small things.

Counselors and administrators are part-time detectives. Most young people are honest, but we also deal with those who lose or conveniently rearrange facts. A good detective seeks those facts closest to the "time and scene of the crime" when memories are more accurate. Educational detectives need to know the facts and be able to act before the student has a chance to call or message home and present a fabricated story about how they were mistreated. Unfortunately, cell phones make beating their message home nearly impossible.

GENERATING SITUATIONAL SUCCESS

No counselor or administrator wants to be blindsided by a parent's phone call about how their student's situation was "mishandled." To avoid this outcome, we need to streamline the inter-school process of communicating with others that a situation exists. But when and where is the best place to address problems? What strategies should be used?

Strategy # 1

It is a productive policy to act before there is a problem to address. Administrators should send phone messages to all parents before the school year starts to establish goodwill and briefly inform the parents that if an incident occurs and is brought to their attention, they will investigate, collect the facts from all involved, and then be in touch.

This olive-branch effort can help clear up any lingering muddy thinking in the mind of parents due to prior-year or administrator encounters when things did not go well. Assure the parents that, as far as you are concerned, every year begins with a clean slate.

Not everything should be in one message. No one wants to read a manual. Tell parents how many messages you will send and when to show that you want to be thorough while respecting the parents' time.

Outlining what will be done to resolve an issue before any problem exists and tempers flare makes the parents feel like partners. Managing behaviors with people who will reasonably work together for the best of their child encourages all to buy in.

The following pages have a two-message sample. You can personalize the message by inserting the names of parents and children.

Parent Communication Template #1

Dear (Parent Name),

The entire staff of (School Name) joins me in looking forward to sharing a successful experience with you this school year. We thank you for the privilege of working with you and each child.

One purpose of summer vacation is to give everyone a break from last year. If your experience with the school was good, plan for it to continue. If there were a few bumps, be assured they are history. Everyone begins the year fresh. Everyone. Discipline files are empty. We want it that way.

We tell students who transfer into our school that they will teach us what they are like. If they had problems at their old school or did not get along with people, that is in the past. They will teach us who they want to become and how they want to be treated. We always start by assuming interactions will be positive and that negatives will be correctable and diminish in number and seriousness. As students get better at following our shared rules, respect and learning increase.

Returning students will also teach us what they will be like this year. Many young people grow up a lot over the summer break, and we welcome the more grown-up attitude and success.

We look forward to working with you and your family to develop a successful school year. I will be sending you a second encouraging message in a few days.

Continued Success,
(Your Name)

Parent Communication Template #2

Dear (Parent Name),

I hope you received my earlier message about the positive relationship we plan to have with you and your student(s) in the coming school year. Here are a few ways we can help each other.

Perhaps you are the lucky parent of students who never do anything wrong, make mistakes, or "forget" the rules. Unfortunately, these things can happen even with the great ones. We ask that if something goes wrong and your student is "in trouble," take their phone call or message with a grain of salt until the adults have communicated.

A teacher cannot stop in the middle of multiple back-to-back courses, nor can a bus driver stop their vehicle in order to get to the root of a situation and gather all the necessary details. Of course, you can contact us at any time, but please take a breath and give us an opportunity to do our due diligence and find out the facts.

Many children relay everything with sincerity except the details that do not favor them. As a parent, you understand this. We are not going to communicate for something simple like a child who needs to be reminded to be quiet unless it happens over and over. As a parent, you have experienced this form of energy.

You want us to have your back to help the children grow into mature adults. We need you to have our backs in helping the students to follow the rules, grow to meet challenges, have a great time, and learn as much as they can.

We work to bring out the best in all children and appreciate the opportunity to work with you to make this everyone's best year.

Continued Success,
(Your Name)

Successful leaders are proactive. By communicating directly and early, you'll show respect for the parents' responsibilities, problems, and desire to help and protect their children. Gaining goodwill puts positive credit in everyone's good-relationship bank account.

If a parent had a bad experience with a prior administrator, the current administrator may now have closed a communication gap that lingered in the parent's mind. Since the bank account is positive, the administrator may be given the benefit of the doubt when the child contacts home to say they were "wronged" at school.

Year after year, positive communications add to an administrator's, counselor's, or teacher's reputation of wanting to work with parents instead of being a cold fish at the end of a negative phone call. No one likes to be contacted only when there is trouble. Instead, build up a positive balance in your communication bank account.

Another opportunity is to send a brief thank-you note to parents before Thanksgiving in the United States. Or send one out of the blue just because you were thinking about how many people are providing such great support.

In addition to parents, students need to be shown that they also have clean slates. Do not assume they know it. Students who have been in trouble or have low self-esteem need to know they are not starting in a hole. Students pick up on words and smiles in the hallway and possibly a message before school starts or at appropriate times during the year.

Strategy #2

People are more motivated to change or correct their behaviors closer to actual events because emotions have not dulled.

Suppose a child breaks something at home. They hope not to be found out. If they can get through the day and night, they feel a little insulated from paying the price. If days pass before the broken item is found, they feel confident enough to say, "It was okay when I saw it last week," because that is the truth. It *was* okay before they broke it.

Most people feel bad when they screw up. They wish it had not happened or that the problem could have been avoided. The old saying that "time heals all" can also apply to feelings of a need to correct unchallenged behavior. Once time passes after making their mistake, people rationalize that the incident must not have been that important. When confronted later, their response might be, "Oh, too bad about that." And the next time they screw up, they may be more willing to let time work its anti-behavior-change magic.

To avoid this type of apathy, administrators and other educators need to move quickly to acknowledge situations and be clear that appropriate actions will be taken. Little or late action calls into question whether those in charge care. Prevent negative opinions held by a few from becoming your reputation. Once lost, it takes work to regain.

Strategy #3

Situations may fix themselves through nothing anyone in the school system did. Yet, indirectly, anyone who tried to help gets partial credit for the cure. People remember those who gave fast acknowledgement of their problems. That builds goodwill and a willingness to pay back later.

Strategy #4

A quick response shows the educator cares, that they are active, responsible, and in charge. It might be as simple as an acknowledgement of an incident. Educators do not need to hear what their regular problems are. Outsiders and insiders tell them all the time.

Excellent administrators prioritize issues while the actors involved are sure their fire is bigger and hotter than those of others. Yet, the person in charge must respect all fires, from tiny embers through blazes. Not recognizing someone's concern is its own fire, and no one needs a double-alarm fire.

To decide which fires to prioritize, use the matrix I've provided in this section to isolate which situations to act on now, let cool, take advantage of while they are hot and ready to build on, and which to monitor. This is not a one-and-done-for-the-year list. Priorities adjust as the school-year seasons flow, so revisit this exercise often to keep addressing what is important.

I encourage you to write down your fires directly in the book, or download the printable form from the *Skills Through Presentations Program* if purchased for use in future evaluation and planning situations. Writing your fires down is a form of containment. Write them big or small depending on whether you are developing or diminishing them. Do not make everything equal. You control what you do to improve the environment.

Keep your mindset above the mud of problems. Mud wears you out. Plant above it. Beautiful things grow there.

Most tropical orchids are epiphytes that grow hanging in the air with no soil. And, at times, be grateful for a problem. It is an excuse or reason to grow a better program.

Fires and Issues Matrix

Fires/Issues to Put Out Now, Let Cool Before Action, Build On, or Monitor

Fires/Issues to Put Out Now	Fired Up Things to Build On
Fires/Issues to Cool Before Action	**Fires/Issues to Monitor**

After documenting the fires or issues you're currently managing, use this matrix to delineate the actors, goals, objectives, steps to take, and resources required to address the fires that need to be put out now.

Fire/Issue: _____

Identified Fire Personnel	Goals and Objectives
First Three+ Steps to Take	Resources Needed

Strategy # 5

Work with the experts. The best people who can point out problems the administrator or counselor faces (or will face) are professionals who share their experiences. It is essential to build a support system to act as a sounding board that is willing to share your problems, tactics, availability of resources, and possible solutions. If it takes a village to raise a child, it takes a village of administrators to raise a school or school system.

At times, the experts are among the rank and file who deal with the problems daily. They may know how to fix part of the issue with simple changes. In this case, you just gained an ally in executing the larger effort.

Students transfer from one school to another for many reasons. At times, the new school should be made aware that the student has had problems with authority, but privacy is important, and we never want to set up a student for failure when they need a second chance. However, if a student might really act inappropriately, that information should be shared so the new school can be prepared — not to catch the student doing something wrong, but to better ensure the student's success. It might make a difference as to which teachers they are assigned to, as certain teachers handle certain types better than others.

A few parents are in complete denial about the faults of their child and would be furious if privacy was invaded — even by the truth. In that case, I might talk to the child's previous counselor or administrator about a related problem and ask how their school deals with it. They may know that I already know about the child in question, even if we're not speaking about them by name. As professionals get to know each other, things can be communicated without stating the problem.

The key to standing up to problems, resolving issues, and prioritizing fires is communicating. Get messages of cooperation out to parents, students, and staff. Know where the fires are, which ones to put out, and which to use to bring the energy.

CALL THEIR BLUFF

Every administrator has had someone complain about an issue to them. If the educator knows the person and their personality, a good tactic may be to call the person's bluff by asking them to serve on a committee to investigate the issue and generate recommendations for appropriate responses for this and similar fires. Often, when the rubber hits the mud, it smothers their interest in that fire. At other times, the person appreciates the vote of confidence and does impressive work. Fire out. Ally gained.

RUBBER BAND LEADERSHIP

Leaders stretch out in front of those they lead while remaining in touch with followers who often are also leaders in the military, businesses, etc. Top leaders go out into areas followers may not consider. That is the leader's responsibility and opportunity.

The leader-follower relationship is shown in my presentation *Rubber Band Leadership,* which has been used at leadership conferences, Student Council events, and in classrooms. During this presentation, an eight-inch-long rubber band is hung between the hooked fingers of the leader and follower. The leader steps away to stretch the rubber band but not so far as to break their relationship. The follower chooses to step forward to keep up and grow in the relationship — or not. The follower then becomes the leader of others as roles, challenges, and nuances of leader-follower relationships mutually develop.

Again, much more detail is available in the full presentation, including the optional two levels of discussion questions and projects developed by using Bloom's Taxonomy.

IT'S THE STUPID STUFF

What really wears on educators is not meeting challenges; it is dealing with and cleaning up the "stupid stuff" people do that creates both real and factiously frustrating problems. As a counselor who frequently served in administrative roles, I remember thinking in too many situations, *You did what?* Usually, this was a reaction to the actions of students, but at times, those of parents, teachers, and staff.

The actions and issues that cause the "stupid stuff" exemplify muddy thinking — or a lack of thinking. We expect this of the young who think two great thoughts forward and a confusing thought backward. Helping them mature increases the odds to four thoughts forward and one step back. That is the challenge and opportunity for educators.

At times, administrators experience the *You did what?* phenomenon with teachers and staff they know should know better. Muddy thinking that often leads to out-of-character action is a result of frustration, miscommunication, or overreaction.

As a result of muddy thinking and action extremes, insecure and suspicious people make things up because they abhor a vacuum. They follow any idea or cause even if little or no clarity is presented. And they like to share. In this way, they're like middle school drama queens. Leaders of fictitious issues may cause turmoil for ulterior motives or because they live in a sea of muddy ideas.

It is impossible for educators to prevent all people from thinking, doing, or saying muddied-up, stupid things, but they can help reduce these situations through clear communication and expectations. If even intelligent people do not know what is going on, they hypothesize plans, reasons, and motives. They muddy things up.

Clarify communications and expectations.

Yes, it can be that simple.

TEACH IT OR COACH IT?

At Creighton Prep in Omaha, Nebraska, I had a two-and-a-half-block walk from my office to the principal's office. In other schools, it was twenty-five feet. Counselors in small schools participate in administrative duties as part of the administrative team. Over the course of my small-school experiences, I was probably in charge of the building for more than a year if you added up all the periods and days. No big deal. The needs of the job came first. Job descriptions slipped to second.

Adopting this mindset of putting the needs of the job above your individual role is one way teachers may need to clear up their muddy mindset. One teacher I worked with thought a new academic assignment he had been given was not important. He was a very good coach, but he did not put the level of effort into the new assignment the students deserved.

I was proud of how this teacher, a great man, responded to my suggestion that he teach this class as if it were his team in a competition where they would have to present what they learned against other schools. He immediately saw not a responsibility but an opportunity. His mindset and product excelled. We lived happily ever after.

Another example involved extracurriculars. In my decades spent as a Student Council advisor, I supervised hundreds of meetings and addressed many groups at workshops and conventions. It was great to work with energetic young leaders. Any good advisor must want to help students get better through activities, but advisors and members need to learn their roles.

I remember a coach who also became the Student Council advisor. He said, "If they want to do something, I will help them. It is up to them." This muddy mindset would never be acceptable when dealing with his athletes. He would never allow his team to decide if they wanted to work out, lift weights, or have hard practices. Athletes want to work to get better to win. They would be confused if the coach did not care enough to challenge them to improve. Student Council members are the same. They deserve to be led or coached. That is the responsibility and opportunity. You get it. Make it happen.

PARLIAMENTARY PROCEDURE READERS THEATER

An easy way to help anyone learn parliamentary procedure is found in *Skills Through Presentations* in the form of a bonus reader's theater play. It teaches the main parliamentary motions by having the participants simply read the actor's parts. It is funny, easy, and effective.

The person in charge hands out the scripts, assigns the parts, and lets the participants read. Participants pay attention because they do not know when their part is coming up. After 25 minutes, they have learned the main motions and have practiced them through a meeting within the fictitious meeting. No teaching or boredom required.

When dealing with educators, there are times when leaders must find the staff's button and not be afraid to push them to help students. Be kind. Be respectful. Be cool. We all want one thing: Outstanding graduates.

At times, we put out the fire, and at times we stoke it. More on this in Chapter 9.

ASPIRE TO TEACH, AFFECT, AND INSPIRE GENERATIONS

Sometimes, students are rolled out the door and into a cold world. If students can do little, they, and the lives of many of their children and subsequent generations, may languish. No one goes into education to help anyone settle for less. Educators are builders who should see their imprint on the lives of students in multi-levels of generational success. Administrators think long-term, and teachers need to think in a generational sense while acting short-term. Growth follows growth and settling for less follows settling for less.

The greatest impact an educator may make is setting the course for a current student that affects the course of that student's very special great-grandchild, who is better positioned to make a difference for society through an invention, discovery, or analysis of a huge problem.

Chapter 3 will mention millions of immigrants who came to a new land to elevate their descendants' lives. When someone from a family that has not worked to achieve higher education goals steps out of the family mud and decides to learn at higher levels, they have crossed the ocean to a land filled with diplomas, degrees, certificates, and opportunities. They work for their family and for their children to continue their growth forever.

All children are important and deserve to be served. The mindsets of the people we work with now may set up the lives of incredibly important and gifted children who will affect generations, even nations. The efforts of educators now may yield Nobel Prize winners in the future. Think greatness.

All children are important and deserve to be served. The mindsets of the people we work with now may set up the lives of incredibly important and gifted children who will affect generations, even nations.

During an educator's career, the inner fires we create in students are more important than the ones we put out. Be proactive with communication and take on the doubters and the stupid stuff. They are the petty change in your goodwill and success bank account.

Appreciating multi-generational successes reinvigorates the big mission and mindsets and increases the energy brought into classrooms. We need people who aspire to inspire generations. Is that you? At times, it is hard, even for the best. Do what great coaches do.

Take a breath. Reset your mindset. Take it one play at a time. You've got this. Now roll!

THINGS TO REMEMBER AND APPLY

o Administrators should message all parents before the school year starts to establish goodwill and inform them that if an incident is brought to their attention, they will investigate, collect facts, and be in touch. Extending an olive branch prevents many high-end emotions from forming.

o Successful leaders are proactive. Gaining goodwill puts positive credit in everyone's good-relationship bank account. Students also need to know they start a year with clean slates.

o People are more motivated to change or correct their behaviors closer to the actual events because emotions have not yet dulled. Act quickly. Situations may fix themselves through nothing anyone in the school did. Yet, indirectly, anyone who tried to help gets partial credit. Quick responses show caring, activity, responsibility, and control.

o Prioritize and categorize what to work on and when and thank certain problems. They are reasons to grow better programs.

o Work with people at or above your level to fix problems but be sure to include people who work with the problems daily.

o Call a complainer's bluff.

o Tell certain teachers to coach a class, not teach it. They will get it.

o The greatest impact an educator may make is to set the course for a student now, that sets the course for their exceptional great-grandchild.

CHAPTER 3

ELEVATING MINDSETS

*It costs so little to teach a child to love
and so much to teach him to hate.*

— FR. FLANAGAN

Everyone wants to have a great mindset, think independently, and acquire information and circumstances of their own choosing. The young make internal choices about the external choices they are stuck with, accept, or are grateful for. They waver between almost thinking they know everything, learning on their own, and accepting adult help to grow.

Adult Intelligence, the original AI, has traditionally been crucial to the development of youthful mindsets. Artificial intelligence, the new AI, will replace part of human adult influence. Humanity has always had people with warped mindsets who misuse their intelligence for selfish gains and illegal activities. Their infestation will expand with the use of AI because AI will inspire or infect almost everything we experience. This shift will mostly be good because when intelligence expands, great things happen.

Trying to place an adult point of view, or mindset, into the mind of a teenager by forceful argument is usually doomed. That may have been the sole parenting technique passed down to certain parents from grandparents and older generations. They use what they know. What they may not know is the huge difference between being an autocrat and being an authority figure. Lectures appear to work when the "lectured to" has no choice but to agree.

Authority figures are authentic if they command and earn, not demand, respect. Everyone will follow authenticity because strength guided by wisdom makes sense. People follow orders, but they will go much further through follow-ups and assistance if the orders make sense. Think about the talk you've heard in the faculty lounge or outside the faculty meeting. Who is on board with the administration?

As with adults, students follow those they respect, not people who are weak and let them get away with things. A teacher can be friendly and authoritative. A teacher cannot want to be the student's best friend. Referring to a teacher who could not control his students, I confidentially asked a great student of mine, James, why he did not behave in this teacher's class. He cut to the core. "We'd behave, but he doesn't make us, so we don't." The same group would leave that room and be respectful of other teachers' directions for the rest of the day.

Students do not respect weakness. They respect the strength of discipline that is fair and usually — but not necessarily — always equal. Circumstances may make outcomes different. Small children do not yet grasp the difference between equality and fairness. If the discipline environment is fair, older students can live with differences.

In the preceding four paragraphs, do you see mindsets everywhere? Here's what I see:

- Parents parroting one strict, authoritarian, disciplinary technique.
- Authority figures who earn and deserve, not demand, respect.
- A teacher who wants to be friends more than they want to be professional.
- Great students acting weakly to take advantage of allowed weakness.
- Great students following the greatness track in other classrooms.
- Teachers who are great at teaching and managing their students.

Some of these mindsets fall into the "stupid stuff" mentioned in Chapter 2. The weak teacher and strict parents were not bad people; they simply needed to elevate their techniques. We need to make obvious changes and raise the mindset of everyone in the school, including parents, teachers, and staff. Bring on the original AI, Adult Intelligence. The sooner we get mindsets elevated, the sooner school and life work better.

For many decades, one of my Catholic schools required one of two versions of a course called Parenting, which was about managing a family. Students explored what it was like to be a parent, live on a budget, take care of a baby, and make a marriage work. (As an aside, it always required the completion of an additional economics or personal business course so students knew how money works and how to take care of personal business. They were incredibly practical.)

Families need that extra mile. Society needs that extra mile of family and Core Values+. Future schools loved to work with those who'd taken the courses. Sadly, the Parenting course was dropped. You know why — budget cuts. At times, savings trumps mindsets.

Each school and society needs to set priorities that are in the best long-term interests of families, students, and citizens. Setting money aside, we have competent educators who do their best in their circumstances. Schools set themselves up to systemize the production of great habits or weak ones. What is acceptable? Live in a great mindset or a messy, muddy mindset. There are programs that can make things better, and they do not cost much.

Young people do not have all the information and techniques they need to survive and thrive, but they do know if they are being informed, handled, or regimented. The only solution is to attract them through wisdom and their own self-interest. At times, we must change educators' mindsets to change students' mindsets.

Skilled teaching presents content and an underlying message, which may be the more important of the two. This form of educating has gone by terms like dual messaging. Going deeper, what intrigues me is the art of teaching without appearing to be teaching. It is often best to affect mindsets when they are not on guard or feel they are being manipulated. Teaching through a growth subtext is where we can help mindsets to evolve.

Inspiring a new thought process can lead to a more sophisticated mindset. True, that may be rationalization, but it is part of my mindset and based on years of seeing this approach work. Do not use a hammer to drive home a message when a feathery thought, floating in the breeze, is better appreciated and accepted. This is very important when trying to win over the thoughts and mindsets of the young. We must stop convincing fragile mindsets that some subjects are hard. We do it all the time.

May we examine the mismanaged mindset that if you understand and are good at math, you are intelligent, and if not, you are not? There is no reason that the Math Club could not be much bigger. I have worked with special needs through almost "genius" math students and every level in between. They all deserve respect and a path to success. If math can help them, then let's get it done.

We can improve math mindsets by convincing people that if they can follow directions, they can do math. Name any subject aside from math that gives all the directions or rules up front all the time. To succeed in math, simply follow the directions. Let's look at two lists of subjects:

We can improve math mindsets by convincing people that if they can follow directions, they can do math. Name any subject aside from math that gives all the directions or rules up front all the time. To succeed in math, simply follow the directions.

MASTERING MIND MUD IN SCHOOLS

Subjects Where All Directions and Rules Are Provided Up Front	Subjects That Have Rules but Do Not Follow Them All the Time
Mathematics	Language Studies
	Science
	Social Science
	Music
	Computer Science
	Theology
	Industrial Arts
	Philosophy
	Family Consumer Science
	Driver's Education
	Political Science
	Foreign Language
	Dramatic Arts

Mindsets about the ability to do math are mismanaged in certain societies, families, and even schools. Certain groups are pre-conditioned to believe they may not be good at math, yet they are still supposed to learn it. How stupid is that? Math is totally honest. It tells us what to do all the time.

Math needs to be presented as the only subject where the rules are a sure thing. Just follow the directions, and you will succeed. Math wants to make students great. Teach children to follow gradually more difficult directions in any subject or area, then, teach math. Teach through flow, not struggle.

True, mathematics is used by some to mislead others, but mathematics is not to blame. It follows its rules. It is people with estranged mindsets who follow their own selfish rules or ways to use math in illegal endeavors or to mislead people. That is a screwed-up mindset.

SLAVERY, A HORROR OF HISTORY

Now we turn to something everyone reading this work and everyone learning in school is united in opposing. Slavery is universally abhorred by caring, loving people who may totally disagree on many other topics. There is no place in modern society for it. 99.9 percent of us are united by this mindset.

Let's examine how muddy mindsets tricked people into thinking that some people were superior, when the muddy thinking was inferior. Throughout ancient and into recent world history, slavery was accepted as a normal state of existence even by the people unfortunate to be slaves. No one wanted to be a slave, but they accepted they were pawns in an established system. For millennia, anyone could become slaves, even teachers and doctors. The mindset of the world's population was set. Nothing was going to change the system, even if some could be freed or buy their freedom.

A person could be free in an ancient spring, but if crops failed and debts had to be paid, the bankers were cold — very cold. That borrower could be a slave in the fall until the debts were repaid. They'd just have to deal with it.

If an ancient country was conquered, that population knew they could become slaves until they revolted and became free. Part of being a conqueror was making sure those conquered would be chained in physical and psychological ways so they would not revolt. Oppressors ruled the mind-sets of the oppressed.

African chieftains sold off warriors from defeated tribes to both make money and maintain control of those who remained in the conquered lands. It is always about money and positioning to increase the grip on power — usually to make even more money.

Slaves were victims of history's mindset missteps. Oppressors do not suppress because they have nothing else to do. They want to increase bottom lines and border lines. Oppressed people were muscle machines. That's it. Nothing personal. You have your mindset. We have ours — plus an army.

At times, race was a card played with slavery. Talking about one race being superior to another was always irrational, but let's never underestimate the power of a good rationalization to affect lower mindsets. They may not want it to be true, but they still believe it or are forced to believe it.

> Slaves were victims of history's mindset missteps. Oppressors do not suppress because they have nothing else to do. They want to increase bottom lines and border lines. Oppressed people were muscle machines. That's it. Nothing personal. You have your mindset. We have ours — plus an army.

Everyone knows slavery for the sake of money and land is wrong, but mankind is morally weak and self-centered. Many races and peoples have paid the price for immoral mindsets. Throughout most of history, those in power in many countries found it easier to convince the population that the real reason for slavery was to control a dangerous, inferior race.

Most countries are past this hurdle, but people in power still understand the importance of mindsets. Because of this, citizens need to know how to avoid being controlled. It is the job of educators to make young minds aware that they must protect themselves from manipulation. Now, manipulation comes from the far end of political parties in many countries, social media, advertisers, etc., as the real manipulators try to throw us off by stating the other group is the real threat.

Does a better understanding of slavery as acceptable in the views of many cultures in history make it more understandable, palatable, or acceptable? No. What if slavery was mentioned as part of life in the Bible? Does that legitimize slavery and diminish the Bible, or are we missing something? Without knowing key points, aspects of any mindset may be wrong. We need to go deeper. Always deeper.

SLAVERY IN THE BIBLE WAS A BUSINESS DEAL

In the Bible, slavery was referenced as controlling others by mental and physical chains, and as being willing to give up everything to be a slave to help others, but in most cases, it referred to a simple business relationship. An acceptable practice in Biblical times was for a poor person to lease themselves to a rich person for seven years, usually to pay off a debt. For example, a parent might lease a child to gain the money needed to plant a crop.

The objective might also be to get into the wealthy individual's good graces in hopes of eventually working for them as a free person. Often, the "slave" was doing the same work they would have done if not a slave, so it was not a big deal. In the seven-year lease, no abuse was allowed. If abuse occurred, by law, the "slave agreement" was ended. It is a little more complicated and not all good, but this is the essence of most slavery references in the Bible.

Should a better word than *slavery* have been used in the Bible or society to describe the loan of one's services? Apparently, no one cared. It was a fact of life, and using another term would not have changed a thing.

Biblical slavery is an example of not understanding another period of human history and the mindset of the people who lived then and in other cultures. They saw, thought, and did things differently than we do today. We like to think we are correct in what we do, but our approach may just be different. It is difficult to change if the mind is set and not open to our human differences of opinion. The disciplined mind must be open to other disciplined minds.

At the time of the Civil War in the United States, owning slaves was a hardline mindset issue that was bigger than the rights of states. The mindsets of slave owners affected real lives in ways it is hard for current minds to imagine, let alone condone.

Many good people attempted to expand our understanding of slavery in that period of US history and its aftermath. Was there any carryover, and how did it affect the decisions of subsequent generations through blatant or subtle oppression?

When considering this, it occurred to me that although I knew more people lived in the North than in the South, I didn't know exactly how many. What was the difference in population? How many people supported slavery in 1860, and how many of them have descendants who currently live in the United States? The answer to the first question is easy to research. The answer to the second can be projected. Why do this in a chapter talking about mindsets? As an example of open and closed mindsets and to open perspectives and reset the accuracy of mindsets.

We know many minds become set based on personal interpretations of history, modern philosophy, psychology, political positions, and even theology. What follows is based on mathematics. There is zero intent to bruise feelings or positions. Facts are facts. Facts affect mindsets. In the following section, you may find some that surprise you. Math can open you to worlds you thought you knew but previously accepted based on arguments from other disciplines.

PEOPLE OPPOSED TO SLAVERY WANT CRITICAL GROWTH

According to the United States Census Bureau, in 1860, 31,433,321 people lived in the 33 states and nine territories of the United States. 18,773,212 lived in the Northern states and most of the territories. 12,600,109 lived in the South, including 3,953,760 slaves. There were some slaves in the North, but too small a number to sway the statistics that follow. About 4,000 slaves, or a tenth of one percent, were captives in the territories. The vast majority of these were in the District of Columbia, which was a territory at the time.[1]

There were probably people in the South who opposed slavery but who were outvoted. There were certainly people in the North or the territories who supported slavery, but the law did not support that view. Those numbers are unknown, so we will assume that, for the most part, they canceled each other out. The numbers used here are from the Census Bureau's records and other credible sources.

The slaves certainly would not want to be included in the group supporting slavery, so when the slave population is subtracted from the total population of the South and added to the people who lived in the North, that total would be 22,726,972 or 72.3 percent of the US population who did not support slavery. Only 8,646,349, or 27.7 percent of the people living in 1860, supported slavery. These percentages might vary slightly after 1860 because of the hundreds of thousands who died on both sides of the Civil War.

If anyone thinks there is a hangover in oppressive thinking that affected more recent history, I understand the theory, but math continues to destroy that position. We will not quibble over a percent or two because any other concerns about the percentages are made negligible by the vast influx of immigrants into the United States between 1860 and 2018, when about forty million or more immigrants were added to the US population. Consider the millions who came to the US around WWI. They did not come to the US to oppress anyone. In fact, many were fleeing oppression.

Next, consider the millions of children of these immigrants who became US citizens at birth after 1860. None of these immigrants or their children can be tied to the era of slavery in the US or inherit latent guilt about it.

If 72 percent of the population in 1860 can be categorized as anti-slavery, and we add 40 million immigrants and generations of descendants to this group, it is mathematically projected that around 90 percent of the current US population has no support for slavery in its ancestry. Few in this group could have carryover guilt based on ancestral support of slavery. If any want to dispute a 90/10 split, accept 10 percent more. 80/20 is too low yet leads to the same conclusion.

My focus is to prepare students for prosperous futures through Core Values+ and skill-based mindsets to maximize schooling for better jobs and lives. The parents of students want better providers for their grandchildren.

As a thought experiment, imagine what slaves would have wanted for their descendants. First, they would have wanted them to control their destiny. They would have wanted them to be able to choose from great career options, not settle for what they have no choice about, which is a form of self-imposed slavery. The ancestral slaves would have wanted descendants who were free of poverty, who could hold their heads high and take care of their families in every way.

REPARATIONS THROUGH HIGHER PAY AND STANDARDS

When this book is read outside of the US, it will not make sense to refer to any racial group as a minority, because every group is a minority somewhere and a majority somewhere. In Chapters 4 and 6, we will address the problem of "minority" students and members from all races not graduating from high school and an unusual way to get through to them. Graduation is the baseline that improves economic bottom lines.

There are movements to pay reparations to Black Americans because of slavery, but there will never be enough money to meet

> Graduation is the baseline that improves economic bottom lines.

the monstrous scope of the crime or to sufficiently address the real needs of millions of people.

The indigenous peoples of the Americas also have a different — but valid — claim. The people of the United States stole everything from the people who lived here before us. There is no fair way of making amends to and for everyone, especially by most of the people currently in the country who had nothing to do with either situation.

There is a better way than paying reparations.

The focus here is on working with young people. The better way to great future paydays for students is to keep them in school as long as possible so businesses will pay them well for doing a great job once they've graduated. In the long run, it will cost taxpayers little because more people will be earning more and paying more taxes. No one will argue against educating people to develop better workers, and the earners gain and maintain self-respect.

I would wager that if the parents of many black children were told to choose between their children graduating from high school and some, or all, of them earning at least a community college degree or getting a one-time reparation check in the mail, the parents would take the first option and call it good. That option is good for parents, their children, and society. Win, win, win.

Older members of minority groups who were oppressed can shift their mindsets and raise their games by accessing educational programs at community colleges or online. A year or two of training in the area the person chooses — carpentry, machine operations, plumbing, hair styling, etc. — can turn into a good living. Employers are waiting, but they do not want people who can barely do the required work. They and their customers require high standards of success and service. The employers deserve quality work if the pay is good. An employee cannot do their job correctly only 50 percent of the time.

Are students really helped even if they graduate but can do little because they barely met low graduation standards in low-level courses? Everyone involved in a student's education must adjust their mindsets to raise reading, math, verbal, and technical skills instead of lowering passing grades and graduation standards. Who really believes the 50 percent passing mark in some schools belongs in education?

If teachers are told by superiors to pass the class, students figure it out and stop working. Who is rationalizing, giving up, caving in, protecting jobs, and abdicating opportunities? I do not put you, the reader, in that category. You would not be reading this material if your mindset was only concerned with keeping your job while graduates passing with a 50 percent are sent into an increasingly complex world, only qualified to do low-level work. It is on educators to hold up standards and for students to step up.

True, certain students face cultural and language difficulties or have tough backgrounds to overcome, but what are we telling employers who do not require or check the applicant's high school transcript? General Education Diplomas allow for high school graduation equivalency. Everyone knows they are legally the same but not the same because the student gave up on high school — even if for a valid reason.

There are state-defined alternative high school diplomas for students with significant cognitive disabilities, but do we also need a different diploma for schools that do not require 70 percent as a passing mark? Would a Basic Education Diploma be more accurate for students who chose that route in a high school that also offers the traditional diploma with higher standards?

Can 70 percent be required for all but five courses that could be set at 50–60 percent as the passing standard? This could be appropriate for a student identified as having poor language skills or who is fine in every subject but math. This diploma could not be applied for after failing the courses. It should not be easy to get and could even be lost if a student does not produce appropriate work in courses that may require special assistance. This alternative could not be an easy out, but it could help.

To make it in the real world, everyone must meet standards. The world's "mindset" does not care about student situations, even if parents and educators do. The reality is that caring is not enough. We must do something, or we are just part of the world's mindset that lets needy students flop in the wind and land where they may. That is a mindset that says, "Good luck. Nice to meet you. We are moving on."

This modified workaround diploma may keep students from dropping out. It may eliminate the 50-percent-to-pass diploma. It would tell the lazy, "You cannot abdicate responsibilities to work. The days of lazy mindsets are over. Step up, or the world will step around you." That's real.

At one of my schools, a student named Shelia would sit in front of the teacher, learn, and demonstrate she could do the math problems and concepts she was being taught. The next day, she would return, but the learning from the previous day would not return with her. It was totally gone. Shelia could relearn it again and demonstrate it, but the next day, it was gone again.

She was a great person who wanted to know the material, but Shelia was not gifted that way. Her mindset was that of achieving success in math, but her mind would not deliver. As a solution, we enrolled her in the easiest math classes that satisfied her graduation requirements, and her teacher tested her on the day she could do the work. Was that fair or right? In the big picture, it was fair for Sheila because her work was average or above in her other courses, and she knew she would never go into a career that required math.

In another setting, I worked with Denise, a talented, intelligent teacher who could not do math beyond arithmetic. Her high school and college math grades were gifts. The schools adjusted to her work. They did not throw out her overall excellent learning achievements and credibility with the single-skill-deficient bath water.

Would either of these examples have benefitted from approaching math as a simply following-clear-directions mindset? I do not think Sheila and Denise would have gained mastery, but they are at the extreme. Most students would benefit.

How do you know what your school or state should do? Think it through and develop a fair system. Do schools really want to defend or follow a flip-a-coin grading system in which 50 percent right and 50 percent wrong is good enough to pass? That is a terrible mindset. In subsequent chapters, I will go deeper into how to help students who want to raise their games. We already have programs for those who barely can.

In all situations, the focus needs to be on educating young people to build skilled futures for themselves, their families, and their descendants. Once on a roll, subsequent generations roll, but many youths may need to change their attitudes toward education to get rolling. We will show them why. They will need mindsets that accept many pats on the back mixed with other forms of motivation.

TEN PERCENT BETTER

In my presentation, *Ten Percent Better,* ten things of equal size (e.g., books) are placed in two stacks of five. One stack represents positive effort; the other is no or little effort. Underperforming students are not going to wake up one day and give 100 percent effort. They must transition to success.

The first 10 percent is both the hardest and easiest to do. The presenter moves one book from the low-effort stack to the positive-effort to show how much better they could be with 10 percent more effort. The stack with six is now not one but two books higher than the other stack.

Another book is moved, showing stacks of seven and three. Then, a challenge is thrown out as the stacks become eight and two. Visuals move mindsets. More unfolds in the total presentation.

This is an example of how presenters can grasp the principle and then go with the flow without additional coaching or material. The full presentation has depth and 10 two-level discussion questions, exercises, and projects. Remember, complexity is the sum of the simplicities that support it.

GET AFTER IT

On our family farm, children contributed. It took my brother, Allen, and me an hour to walk two miles to bring the cattle into the pens to be safe at night, feed other cattle and hogs, gather eggs, and finish our other chores. Fifteen or more minutes could easily be added to the job if we worked slowly. The pay was always the same: Nothing. We learned to get after it, to work fast and efficiently before it became too dark to play the seasonal sport.

Working fast and effectively is a mindset today's youth need to learn to survive and advance. We must teach and model it, or many will never get it. Many low-achieving students need to learn to get after their studies. I do not mean rushing through the material in the shortest amount of time. I mean learning to stay on task without distractions. Slow studying is not necessarily effective. It robs time from more in-depth study and review.

Let's tie points together. Family farmers were not paid by the hour but by effort. They got after it. In those Iowa summers, before the age of air-conditioned cabs on tractors, I encountered Caucasian farmers with deep, dark suntans that were often darker than many people of color. If the farmers pulled up a sleeve, they might reveal snow-white skin. The different colors on these friends and family made no difference to any of us.

Racial differences are a learned fallacy resulting from weak mindsets. As I shared earlier in this chapter, many decades ago, a part of society implied skin color made a difference. Another part said it did not because behaviors really count. Do people assess a person's value based on skin color or on behavior? White farmers changed color with

Do people assess a person's value based on skin color or on behavior? White farmers changed color with the seasons, so skin color never made sense to me. Behaviors rule. People are people. All races have good, bad, crazy, funny, stupid and brilliant people.

the seasons, so skin color never made sense to me. Behaviors rule. People are people. All races have good, bad, crazy, funny, stupid and brilliant people.

A segment of society keeps digging up racial issues while most people want to move on. The digging taught a younger me to wonder if there was any difference between races. The answer is obvious once an open-minded person spends time with other races. Can we then put slavery to bed? Can we put an end to the thoughts, actions, and mindsets of victims and oppressors? Unfortunately, there is more to the story. Get ready to be uncomfortable.

MODERN SLAVERY

Actual slavery exists in our "modern" world. According to the Global Slavery Index (GSI), there are approximately 50 million slaves on earth today.[2] There is no legal definition of modern slavery, but usually included are forced marriages, debt bondage, sex trafficking, etc. Women and children are the largest groups in modern slave labor. Sex plays an obvious role, but smaller hands are often needed in cramped spaces. Old slave muscles do not move the world now except in less-developed countries. If interested, you can download a three-hundred-page report from the GSI website, which gives extensive details, only a few of which are mentioned here.

Want to be sick? According to the report, there are more than a million modern slaves in the "land of the free." The open southern border of the early 2020s gave this number a boost, especially in sex trafficking and stolen, bought, and sold children.

Border Patrol officers reported that men frequently walked up to the border carrying a child who looked nothing like them because having a child has made it easier to get into the US for decades. The Border Patrol identified more than 6,200 fraudulent family members in fiscal year 2019.[3] In the early 2020s, after they were processed in, many of the children became part of the hundreds of thousands of children the government could not locate.

Many schools do not check the immigration status of those who come to their doors. They see their function as serving the community, not as an extension of law enforcement. It is the ones who do not make it to school that educators are most concerned about.

Want to be sicker? The United States leads the G20 world in importing "at risk goods." These are materials like electronics that are at least partially made by modern slave labor. The US buys more than the next five highest countries put together.[4]

While honoring ancestors, it is time to get the educational emphasis on the right page to protect people who are alive instead of continuing to focus on events from the deep past no one alive played a part in. We cannot change the past, but we can affect the present. Get into a now mindset. If you want to affect these travesties, ask governments to crush modern slavery, which is, unfortunately, everywhere.

I used slavery to show that sometimes it is necessary to expose what we thought we knew in a new light. Mindsets can help or confine us. If mindsets never evolve, people will live mostly in the past. We must push and encourage all mindsets to grow.

STEP OUT OF THE BOX

Here is a glimpse of another presentation. In *Step Out of the Box,* the presenter shuffles around with their feet in two empty cardboard boxes. Inside are invisible worries, problems, etc. Everyone in the audience can see that muddy thinking is slowing this person down. After a few minutes of discussing problems that we carry around, like mistreating or abusing others, the presenter shifts mindsets and kicks the boxes — and their problems — away.

The exercise is easy, impactful, and catches imaginations. This presentation, like most, can last five minutes or 45, if any of the optional questions and exercises are utilized.

THINGS TO REMEMBER AND APPLY

o Adult Intelligence, the original AI, has traditionally been crucial to the development of youthful mindsets — and still is.

o Authority figures are authentic if they earn respect. Students will not follow weak people.

o Schools systemize the production of great habits or weak ones.

o Dual messaging involves the art of teaching without appearing to be teaching. It affects mindsets when they are not on guard or feel manipulated.

o Anyone who can follow directions can do math. It is the only subject that follows its rules all the time.

o For most of human history, slavery was accepted as the way things were. Race was gradually linked with slavery. In the Bible, slavery was referenced as mental and physical chains, but usually, it referred to a non-abusive, seven-year lease. Let go of past slavery. Millions still suffer from it today. Help them.

o The best way to repair the past is to keep students in school as long as possible so businesses will pay them for doing great jobs.

o Does a 50 percent passing mark belong in education? Can graduation standards be high with exceptions in a content area? Students must get after it. That is the way of the world.

A GENTLE SUGGESTION

Would you consider helping students in schools you will never visit or know about? If you learned from this book, please give it to a colleague or buy the inexpensive eBook on Amazon so you can write a brief review about how it helped you. I priced the eBook very low so more students can grow.

Your effort may move others to learn from this book and help students who will never know your name but who will gain from your small kindness because you moved someone to help them.

Be part of a growing mindset.

Be part of the synergy.

CHAPTER 4

WHAT DOES IT CO$T? TOO MUCH NOT TO ACT

The only limits to the possibilities in your
life tomorrow are the buts you use today.
— LES BROWN

We demonstrate our real values through what we do at work, in the home, and when interacting with others. Life is integrated. When valuable aspects of life are not integrated, problems arise. Everything costs something — usually time, money, or stress. In tough times, mindsets need to be strong. That does not happen by accident. We need to prepare no matter the inconvenient co$t.

No person ever said, "I wish I was dumber, poorer, and clueless." But they do, at times, need to be led to and through the work of growing their awareness, mindsets, and skill levels. Educators are in a great spot to help.

Students must have their curiosity met with the truths and nuances of life that educators know best through their Adult Intelligence. While certain students think they know better, some set their minds too soon. Again, am I talking about students or the young through well-aged educators? Everyone, including me, must keep their mindset open.

Decades ago, in my books *Challenging College* and the *Challenging College Workbook*, I had students write down careers they could think of that required two, then four, years of college. The average of fifteen listings showed that the students did not know the expanse of available opportunities.

To raise their games, students must be led, taught, and given opportunities to practice research. At times, the young must be force-fed the information because, though they think they know, they often cannot demonstrate what they know or even what they need to know. We test students in courses, but we also need to evaluate their knowledge of careers and higher education. Without those exams, students may leave school unprepared to significantly advance. Exposing students to potential careers can energize their minds to do more research into what they may really enjoy and can be paid well to do.

Educators want to pay the price to help students. School personnel

> We test students in courses, but we also need to evaluate their knowledge of careers and higher education. Without those exams, students may leave school unprepared to significantly advance.

have unlimited dreams on limited budgets. Everyone in education rides this well-beaten, nearly dead horse that keeps on bucking.

Where do educators get the money for the bonus programs they think they cannot afford? Transforming schools transforms students, which can transform budgets. Elevated mindsets reduce time, money, and talent spent on repeat-offender negatives like absenteeism, discipline issues, justified and unjustified complaints, poor performance in subjects, make-up work, conferences, course retakes, and phone communications. How much could be saved if summer school retakes were cut by a third? It is possible, but it will not happen if steps are not taken to change mindsets and motivate underperforming students.

No student wants to fail, be disciplined, or be destined to make little money in low-end, default jobs. The problem is that some do not know they are stuck in the mud and can get out until a higher power kicks them in their mindset.

Everyone wants to aspire, but some do not know how. It is not obvious, or it would happen to all, all the time. Great educators lead, expose, and herd students to resources and encourage the young to practice courage by taking one step after another to climb their personal educational mountain. That mountaintop morphs into a steppingstone to a sprawling land with plenty of room for all if the educational climbers are prepared.

Attitude toward the journey means almost everything. No mountain climber starts with a weak mindset. They believe they will achieve. Successful climbers do not start the journey with poor equipment, and likewise, students should not start with poor courses and grades. No climber ascends without a plan. Climbers on great slopes have guides to ensure safety. Anyone ascending an educational mountain seeks the advice of the wise. All physical climbers prepare what they will need. Learners pack skills to advance. Climbing physical and educational mountains is challenging, not impossible. Ascending physical mountains gets harder the higher the climber goes. Ascending educational levels can get easier because learners are climbing what they choose to climb. Keep climbing — one foot, one lesson after another.

In the prime climbing season, it costs tens of thousands of dollars to climb Mount Everest because of required permits, equipment, etc. Not everyone can afford it. It costs thousands to ascend higher education, but the means are available in the US through grants and loans. It costs more *not* to be educated, both in dollars and lost smiles from children who may be wanting.

I like two-year degrees that focus on what the student really wants to learn. I understand the theory behind the arts and sciences philosophy of training minds to think diversly and apply that skill to all subjects. But, in a sense, it isn't done because students usually only get a taste of their major in the early years of their degree. They must take courses they may not like before they can take classes on the topics they do like. And we wonder why some drop out.

Why is the key ingredient of their degree being "slow rolled" out? Why do we postpone engaging their enthusiasm for learning? The mature mind understands the arts and sciences view of applying diverse thinking to the subject matter, but not everyone attending college has gained a mature mindset. Because of this delayed enthusiasm, poor study habits, unfortunate circumstances, and immaturity, most campuses lose the equivalent of a full dorm of students by the end of the first semester.

In one of my high schools, I had students at the age and grade level who qualified for geometry but failed the class. The next year they passed the class because it was a second run, their mindsets were determined, and their brains evolved to be able to do abstract thinking. They grasped the concepts, rules, and theorems.

All minds and mindsets do not follow the same growth formula so we must be sophisticated in helping mindsets to grow. When working with groups, educators repeat and reinforce concepts because certain students are not ready for the topic until the second or third time it is shared.

On the other end of the spectrum, I also had young students who took calculus years before they were "supposed" to. Static formulas seldom work for everyone. It takes work to make the system work, but that is our challenge and opportunity. We cannot always work miracles, but the effort is worth it, and at times, miracles happen.

For decades, I built master schedules and walked the walk of setting up opportunities and trying to integrate out-of-the-box course growth. On a few occasions while at Archbishop Bergan Catholic Schools in Fremont, Nebraska, I had students who were also taking courses on two college campuses at nearby Midland Lutheran College and at Metropolitan Community College in the same semester.

Potential dropouts may not be interested in online academic courses, but there may be more options in your area that would intrigue them. It is not easy, but it is rewarding when it works. It may not work this year, but next year, it may be a blessing. Distance education opens the world. We take victories when we can get them.

While writing this, higher education institutions in the United States have their toes draped over the "enrollment cliff" as the rates of high school graduates — their potential students — have begun to decline. Every high school has a group of potential applicants who are not thinking about how higher education could help develop their lives. Elevating educational mindsets can eliminate dropouts, uplift graduates, and supply colleges with needed "replacement" applicants. Eliminated dropouts and high schools, colleges, and society all win.

I spent decades immersed in college admissions and could spend pages discussing the enrollment cliff, but obsessing with a problem may divert us from a solution or partial solution that is staring at us. Benjamin Franklin said, "We are continually faced by great opportunities brilliantly disguised as insolvable problems." A problem is only a problem if we do not act to fix it. It is easier to introduce the solution than it is to have higher education face cutbacks and firings.

High-end educators need to keep their mindsets flexible while maintaining high standards. Colleges must sell the belief that they are setting students up for success. Do colleges want more graduates? Higher education is an open market. Students do not have to

> Benjamin Franklin said, "We are continually faced by great opportunities brilliantly disguised as insolvable problems." A problem is only a problem if we do not act to fix it.

buy in. Middle and high school educators understand this when it comes to selling higher education, but do they understand it when it comes to selling themselves? They must also sell their worth to potential dropouts and lower-end students who are hesitant buyers. I will strongly address this necessity in Chapter 9.

We do not live in a world full of logic and reasoning. We live in a world of social media reasoning. Educators must raise the game. Unsuspecting students don't know what they don't know. Stand up. Save and promote lives.

Students will sit in a rut of muddy thinking if no educator, administrator, or school program gets them moving in a growth direction. These students do not see clearly what adults see as obvious. We have AI, Adult Intelligence. They have their version of AI, Apathetic Intelligence. None of these students wants to be a victim of their own muddy thinking, but they *are* stuck in it. Thankfully, not one of them must stay there. Yet, many will stay stuck unless the school takes more positive action.

Consider the costs put on society by dropouts:[5]

- Every year, dropouts from the graduating class cost the US hundreds of billions in lifetime lost earnings, unrealized tax revenues, and programs to help them. Multiply this by 40–50 years of dropouts, and the overall loss may run into the trillions.
- Students from low-income families are more likely to drop out than those from middle-income families and much more likely than those from high-income families.

- Most inmates in federal and state prisons are high school dropouts. People in tough situations may take chances and do what they would normally not do.
- Median incomes are lower for dropouts.
- Unemployment is higher for dropouts.
- Death rates are higher for dropouts than for graduates.
- Many dropouts could at least be community college graduates.

At times, success follows maintaining positive momentum. If we accept this, then the opposite must be true. We need to interrupt muddy momentum. Action now will save society a great deal in the form of lower crime, law enforcement needs, unemployment checks, social worker interventions, and divorce rates. Saved graduates will pay more taxes at higher rates and help build society.

Look at failure statistics at your school. Look at success rates. Even when success rates are good, all educators want them to be higher.

Everyone in the school can, should, and must be uplifted. A student does not have to be failing to make a significant leap forward. We want to help every student. Everyone can advance. That is the goal, potential, and promise of transformative education.

A relatively small investment in money and time can reduce the repeat-offender problems listed above. The following are seven themes we want students to be freed from or excel in so they, their families, and society can accelerate to greatness.

THEME 1: TOO IMPORTANT TO LOSE – LIFE, HEALTH, AND SAFETY

Current US statistics on suicides are easily available from sources like the Centers for Disease Control and Prevention.[6] Numbers are important, but not as much as the real people walking the halls in schools.

There are several ways to protect life and limb. The best way is to be preventative. To learn how to do this, I recommend accessing the free presentation *Bad Year, Great Life*, available at neilfeser.com, which has proven to change the perspective of many youths slumming in a preoccupation with the bad times of their life.

Of course, saving a life is the first objective and worth the time spent on any intervention. Saving a life saves hours in grief counseling and the attention post-suicide counseling and communication with the many parties takes. The saved time can be spent in productive ways to help those considering suicide and others to have great lives. Action makes it an easy, economical investment.

Many students find it too easy to get involved in drug and alcohol misuse. Problems are not preventable for everyone, but they can be for many. Acting early is the key. It is easy to see how these can muddy up mindsets and thinking.

For current statistics on teenage abuse of illicit drugs, which includes misusing prescription medications or household products, and other health issues, there are many sources of current information, such as the US Department of Health and Human Services and within it, the Office of Population Affairs.[7]

Attendance improves when students have fewer distractions and want to be in school. Attitudes improve and learning increases. It all works better if action is taken to make the atmosphere outside and inside their minds better. This also is the result of eliminating or easing emotional issues such as stress.

THEME 2: MENTAL AND EMOTIONAL ISSUES

Obviously, young people experience mental and stress issues and may compound them with substance abuse. Young people either feel supported or, unfortunately, do not.[8] What can your school do to fill in the gaps and help provide the social-emotional support students need?

Most young people are going to get married someday. Although they will be different than who they are today, everyone is "married" to their future self. If people are going to live as their future selves forever, no divorce allowed, they had better develop a great relationship with their inner mindset and take great care of the future selves. That means taking care of physical and social-emotional needs now. No beating themselves up inside over stupid things their future self will not even remember.

What is being done now that is in their future self's best interests? Are they eating properly and exercising to sustain a great life? Are they studying subjects to learn, or are they preoccupied with social media? Do they want their future selves to be outstanding? Of course, they do. So, how do we best help them?

Educators can keep students' minds on the subject matter by addressing issues that pull minds away. It is worth their — and your — time to address a variety of topics through group work. Often, one or more of those present will be experiencing the issue. There is always a mindset that needs to be growing. By learning how to handle one emotional issue, students gain experience to lean on when the next emotional situation arises. Mindsets benefit from a transference of skills.

All, especially the young, face social-emotional issues, situations, and challenges. Maturity and good mental health come through learning how to transcend issues instead of remaining trapped in a victim mindset. Certain students will not look for help, but if those students are present for a group presentation on dealing with issues, they will pick up ideas and internalize how to help themselves or see the wisdom in seeking personal help. Group work teaches without singling people out.

> Maturity and good mental health come through learning how to transcend issues instead of remaining trapped in a victim mindset.

THEME 3: INTELLIGENCE MUST BE REAL, NOT ARTIFICIAL

Artificial intelligence, AI, will help all of us immensely in many areas, such as in researching cancer cures and analysis of great amounts of data. It will be great if it does not become the equivalent of the drug of choice and take over the thinking processes because then we forfeit our ability to think, reason, and create. We have been down that road before. AI may not be addictive, but it can seriously affect mental development.

We are the best form of intelligence. AI will help everyone to do their work, but if students abdicate their thinking and work skills to AI, why would any employer need, hire, or keep them? The employer would simply ask AI to do the work and skip paying the AI-dependent employee's salary.

AI does not have a mindset because it requires a human mind to enter the race. It is a way to analyze and produce very quickly, which is why it can appear to be intelligent. AI is a tool we need to use wisely. We also need to be cautious and wary of people who will use it against us for their own greed. The dangers of social media are going to be accelerated through AI. All of us need to be wary of what we may not see coming.

THEME 4: RAISE THEIR GAME ACADEMICALLY AND SOCIALLY

No one is born with every skill, attitude, and mindset they need to be successful. People have cognitive potential and emotional intelligence at different levels. It is the job of parents and educators and, at times, the village to elevate each person to reach their potential. However, sometimes the village — now the extended, social media village — is not helpful.

Too many parents are stuck in the mud of extra bills or hard jobs and if others are unable to do as they would like, schools are expected to address the uncovered needs of children. Schools have the choice of ignoring situations or trying to make lives better. In almost every case, schools choose action.

Students need to stay on task and not make excuses. They need to learn how to create and to lay out and follow great paths that stretch them. Many need to raise their academic energy levels. Others may need to develop the courage to overcome self-created fears. All students need to be exposed to how to do these things because most will encounter them somewhere on their journey.

THEME 5: ELEVATE VISIONS, GOALS, SKILLS, AND OPTIONS

Students need to broaden and raise their mindsets, their visions of who they can become, and what they can do. They must learn how to set goals and develop means to attain them. This requires the development of appropriate skills. All of this is aimed at graduating and, if possible, continuing education in their field of interest.

The graduation rate at your high school is what you care most about, but if you want to know how it compares to other schools in your state or the nation, go to the National Center for Educational Statistics website. There, you can research international comparisons and a variety of breakouts and breakdowns.

The most recent statistics as of this writing state that the graduation rate of public schools in the United States is 87 percent.[9] Private schools count graduates whenever they graduate. Public schools count them as graduates if they finish four years after they enter high school. I prefer the private school method. It does not change the mission. Reduce dropouts and elevate all graduate mindsets and success.

If you type "dropouts" in the search bar on the National Center for Educational Statistics website, you'll find many research statistics and tables with a racial breakdown of dropouts. Unfortunately, in 2022, American Indian/Alaska Native (9.9 percent), Hispanic (7.9 percent), and Black (5.7 percent) are the three groups with the highest dropout rates.[10]

Is it a factor of the four-year measuring stick that the graduation rates for all races differ from their dropout rates? Young Blacks in the same tables graduate at a rate of 81 percent, while their dropout rate is 5.7 percent. The remaining 13.3 percent has something to do with the four-year graduation timing of counting students as graduates. I do not care. Graduation rates should be 95 percent or greater, and the dropout rate should be 0.5 percent. We all want the young to succeed.

On the positive side, graduation rates have been gradually rising. It is because schools have done a better job. But questions arise about simply making graduating easier, such as lowering grade percentages required to pass courses or offering easier paths to graduation. This matter has been explored in detail by several groups. You know if standards or graduation options changed in your school and can judge those results. More on eliminating dropouts in Chapter 6.

THEME 6: TRANSFORM BULLIES, BYSTANDERS, AND VICTIMS

Reasonable people do not support or accept abuse. We need to double down on doing everything we can to eliminate all forms of abuse. It is important to change the mindsets of bullies, victims, and bystanders.

Bullies have skills, but their mindsets misuse or abuse the skillsets to the detriment of victims. If not addressed and challenged to change, bullies will continue to use what has worked for them in the past.

Victims have rights and strengths they have yet to develop. They need help in building up their confidence and awareness that bullies base their strengths on fiction. Victims do not have to build their lives on fiction.

Bystanders are incredibly powerful as a group. In a school, they can easily handle bullies by overwhelming them with sheer numbers. They need to realize their power, step out of the mud holding them back, assert their might, and create a better atmosphere in their school for everyone.

I do not want to preach to the choir. If interested in statistics on bullying and other issues, there are many studies and sources, including the School Crime Supplement (SCS) to the National Crime Victimization Survey and the Pew Center Study titled, *9 facts about bullying in the U.S.*

THEME 7: DEVELOP LEADERS AND INTELLIGENT CITIZENS

Everyone is a leader *and* a follower. Unless a person is a loner, both positions are impossible to avoid. Who will be successful in each role? People will fail in handling many opportunities if they are not properly taught the importance of leading and how to step up.

We need people to build up skills in both areas so they can first lead themselves, then lead within the family, at work, and in communities. We need to lean on each other and then work together on challenges. We need to follow the lead of others who know more or have expertise or understanding we do not.

Life is a team effort. Going alone often goes nowhere. Becoming great leaders and followers is like the overused but appropriate imagery of a snowball rolling down a hill. Someone's mindset must get it going. Educators are in the perfect spot to give the snowball the push it needs. When many can lead and follow, everything keeps moving as people take turns, and growth becomes synergistic.

As I have written in other areas of this book, we coach the young and each other to greatness as leaders and followers. In the process, we get better at it ourselves.

THEMES OF SKILLS THROUGH PRESENTATIONS

If you believe the seven themes listed in this chapter should be addressed, consider the *Skills Through Presentations* program because those are the themes to which the one hundred and twenty presentations are assigned. All presentations can be incorporated into the curriculum, Homeroom, etc.

Lists of specific academic departments and numerous topic suggestions for immersion are provided. The presentations can be taught across the curriculum. Sample insertion points into classes like Social Science are provided.

A school does not have to do all one hundred and twenty presentations to be impactful. For example, if four individuals or aggregates of teachers do one presentation per month for ten months over the course of three years, all 120 presentations will be shared. Students get one per week from different directions and voices that tie their real life to academic subject matter. Everything gets real as many problems are addressed, and the curriculum is tied to their real lives as mindsets grow.

However, no school will ever be that symmetrical. Use the presentations when and where they work. Your six-semester sequence may be 28, 23, 22, 15, 16, and 16 to reach all 120 presentations or less because not all have to be used to be very effective. The number and time must fit your school. Schools cannot anticipate exactly when help is needed. Do your best to fit opportunities.

There is so much more in the full program. It is based on decades of in-the-trenches work, which was developed and revised until it fully serves you. And many presentations are fun to do.

THINGS TO REMEMBER AND APPLY

o No person ever said, "I wish I was dumber, poorer, clueless." But at times, they will have to be led to and through the work of growing their awareness, mindsets, and skill levels. Many students who could go on to post-secondary education do not think in those terms.

o Many students sit in a rut of muddy thinking if no person or program gets them moving to make significant leaps forward. That is the goal, potential, and promise of transformative education.

o The best way to save a life is to prevent its loss. You have access to the free presentation titled *Bad Year, Great Life* at neilfeser.com.

o We are the best form of intelligence. AI helps, but if students abdicate their thinking and work skills, why would an employer hire them? Students need to broaden and raise their mindsets and visions of who they can become and learn how to set goals and develop means and skills.

o Bullies have skills, but they wallow in mindsets that misuse or abuse them to the detriment of victims. If not addressed and challenged to change, they will keep using what, unfortunately, works for them.

o Living is a team effort. Going alone may lead nowhere. Becoming great leaders and followers is like the overused but appropriate imagery of a snowball rolling down a hill. Someone's mindset must get the ball rolling.

o Educators can keep students' minds on the subject matter by addressing issues that pull minds away. The seven themes outlined in this chapter match those in the *Skills Through Presentations* program.

CHAPTER 5

GROWTH THROUGH PROCESS

As corny as it sounds, the power of positive thinking goes a long way. So determination and positive thinking combined with talent combined with knowing yourself, your craft...that may sound like a naïve point of view, but at the same time, it's worked for me, and it's worked for all my friends — so I have come to believe it.
— GEORGE LUCAS

We use the term mindset, yet we know the mind is never set. Instead, it is in constant motion. To quiet its motion, people take mental breaks, play, meditate, go on retreats, do activities requiring complete physical attention, or sleep. But even when quiet, it is actively dreaming and creating in the background. Better there than slogging in the muddy ground of worry, regret, depression, or stress. We especially do not want minds slogging through school.

It can be argued that the mind is a set of many things, but that is for philosophers and psychologists to define. Our role as educators is to guide minds in positive directions, no matter the definition of what we are directing.

Without productive methods, we may flounder. Not everyone can articulate their process, which may partially explain why everyone is not consistently effective in what they do. A scientist may not know the answers being sought, but the steps being taken are fully known. Mindsets lead and follow processes to be effective. The scientific method is not the "scenic method," where researchers randomly try anything to see what happens.

Here, I will detail a four-step process I find effective in dealing with problems and opportunities and fulfilling my mission statement and mindset of striving to "improve the flow of success."

This success process includes:

1. Ease, Don't Squeeze
2. Mover Maps, Not Mud Maps
3. Act, Plan, Act
4. Assess, Adjust, Advance

These can be called steps, but I prefer flows. The world's movers and shakers follow their own version or process, which will include some form of these four flows. At times, the success process is a linear flow, while at others, it seems to be a swirl of activity. We may complete the four flows in a matter of minutes or in a different order. Life is not one-size-fits-all. Flows may happen at the same time, or, as in medical emergencies, many flows may play out in seconds. There are times to roll and times to be patient while steadily moving forward.

There is truth to allowing life to happen, but that is not what to tell the boss. To advance successfully, awareness is required, followed by action. Little greatness happens to the unaware. The world never waits for them.

Low achievers often lack true awareness and do not try to link successes together. It appears their process is the easier way of letting life happen to them. That may be part of the path to enlightenment but not to promotions and bigger paychecks. There is a time for enlightenment and a time for work.

The good news is that, like athletic skill sets, the more we practice the process, the more it becomes routine. Routines become easier, automatic, and authentic parts of the way we actively live. Students need guidance in how to grow into them.

Educators must exemplify and teach how to get and stay on a roll. That is what effective leaders do. Every student in a school should have the goal of being an effective leader in their personal, family, work, and community lives. For those who believe, add spiritual life to the list. If any think significant success is not realistic for everyone, many school mission statements should be revised and toned down. A school's mindset should mirror its mission statement. Elevate the mission statement to reality for graduates, or admit that it is just PR to impress, not impact. Walk the walk or settle for talking the talk.

A school's mindset should mirror its mission statement. Elevate the mission statement to reality for graduates, or admit that it is just PR to impress, not impact. Walk the walk or settle for talking the talk.

In schools, things act and interact simultaneously. Those who roll find they can get things done to gain time to simply be. It is a breakthrough when a person can simply be, while energetically getting things done. It is a mindset. You can calmly handle much more than you think you can. I used to joke with one secretary about staying five minutes ahead of the pack. They do not know it, so do not show it. You got this.

It is necessary for good mental health to detach from the stress of the educator's workload. The work is what is done for others. Model that for students who must see that they are not their problems. They may live with problems but not within problems. They may not realize that they have choices, and one is to not internalize problems.

The proper mindset has perspective. It is not set in stone, mud, or blood. Division of processes allows us to enjoy life, get the work done, and not tear ourselves apart. How do we do that?

FLOW #1: EASE, DON'T SQUEEZE

It is not difficult to help people who want help and know what's in their best interests. The challenge is to help those who do not know what is best for them or who think an easier path is more attractive. Ease does not mean easy. It means moving forward with confident wisdom and not squeezing the mind with muddy distractions, worry, and stress.

Helping to clear up known or unknown muddy thinking requires common sense and craft to ease people into wanting to grow. Ordering, arguing, requiring, and pleading have seldom worked in families or schools.

Ordering and requiring does work at first in places like the military, but this must transition to the soldiers buying into the system and taking pride in it. People sitting in classrooms and standing in the front of them work toward goals when they see the truth of what is in their best interests. Students accelerate once they buy in. The alternative is to go out the door and just keep wandering.

Here, the discussion revolves around helping students. Most young people want help, even if they will not admit it. The problem may be that they do not know exactly what, where, and when they need help. Anyone can get the easy students to graduate. It requires a dedicated educator to help the challenging students get to graduation and hopefully go higher. When facing challenging attitudes, as, the saying goes, it is time to "cowboy up!" The opportunity to turn on the light in the tough ones is why many went into education.

Everyone is a student — or should be. Older educator-students may self-apply these lessons while never being too proud, afraid, or embarrassed to ask for help. To stop learning is to stop living.

Every mindset needs a plan. Even better, every mindset is a flowing plan. Every educator needs to be in control without those in their care feeling controlled. That comes when students respect the direction the teacher is taking them. Students want to be in control. Having a plan helps them to feel in

> Every mindset needs a plan. Even better, every mindset is a flowing plan.

control and find their way to their best future. It is the role of educators to teach students how to educate themselves and find their way.

If schools believe in their mission statements and identified objectives, they should actively systematize the implementation of school-wide academic and social-emotional skills growth that students need to develop. Mindsets do not develop without effort and plans.

First, educators must plan the planning process. Use the following forms to develop what is needed by all, then what will be targeted and addressed at specific grade levels. Within the needs of the schools or grade levels, identify the concepts that need to be set as priorities.

Identify School-Wide Academic and Social-Emotional Needs and Skills Students Need to Develop

Academic Needs	Social-Emotional Needs
Academic Skills	**Social-Emotional Skills**

Identify Important Academic and Social-Emotional Needs and Skills Educators Want to Help Their Students Develop in Grade _____ .

Academic Needs	Social-Emotional Needs
Academic Skills	**Social-Emotional Skills**

Identify Important Academic and Social-Emotional Needs and Skills Students Will Need to Develop Soon

Academic Needs	Social-Emotional Needs

Academic Skills	Social-Emotional Skills

FLOW #2: MOVER MAPS, NOT MUD MAPS

Travelers and trackers relied on significant land markings to find their way around the country. Eventually, paper maps helped them get around better and lay out a plan and timetable before leaving.

Many young people barely know about those days. They look up maps online or have their phone tell them where and when to turn. It is easy — until the battery runs out.

As a teen, I remember driving on country roads in a very dense fog. I stopped at an intersection, and my father, who was sitting beside me, said, "Turn north." I just looked at him. Did he know from experience or great instinct? Adults are better at both. Apps can help by supplying leads, but life does not come with an app to discern decisions about careers, aspirations, and social-emotional development. We still are humans, despite the proliferation of apps that tell us they can help with everything. Youth need help in getting out of their "fogs."

A career exercise I used with students had them hypothesize where they would be and what they would be doing in their upcoming decades. Most could imagine where they would live, their career, and whether they were married or not in their twenties, but foreseeing their thirties was hard. Forget the forties and beyond. It was eye-opening for them and reminded me about the importance of being proactive and having them stretch into a much larger future beyond next week or month.

Unfortunately, too many adults settled, rather than found what was truly the best career for themselves.

Too often, people do not broadly search for the right path, or they wait until it is too late to look. As educators and administrators, it is our role to not allow any student to operate from a restrictive set of options. Students want great advice. They want to be movers, not "mudders." We educators know what to do, and it feels great to do it.

Counselors and teachers must take the fight to their students, who do not have a full field of vision. Many do not know what they need to know. We must help them create great potential maps and see themselves as moving on the maps into their best future, or they will flounder and follow muddy ones.

Thankfully, career and school selection searches help students identify starting points. To get to where a person wants to be and become takes effort, but it does not have to be hard. We need to convince the shy and scared that almost everyone has been in their shoes. It will work out, but it will work out much better if they do significant shopping and lay out healthy maps in several directions as options. It is better to have too many choices than only one.

FLOW #3: ACT, PLAN, ACT

If we see a person fall, our mindset is to immediately help them — no agenda required. If someone's academic performance, self-esteem, personal safety, prospects, etc., need help, educators act immediately. We also establish a plan of ways to assist at appropriate times. Then, we act at those times to follow the plan.

Another interpretation is to act, prepare a plan, and then actively engage in its execution. Consider a coach preparing for their next game. The first act they take is to lay out a game plan. Then, they act on it by preparing the team. A defensive player has prepared for what might happen, but the player does not know what the other team will do until it happens. At that point, the player reacts, plans, and acts in a fraction of a second, or it will be too late.

In other situations, such as achieving a peace treaty or building a highway system, the process may take years. Nothing is set. We learn the process and adapt to situations.

It is the educator's job to actively construct a plan to help students. It is the educator's opportunity to model the process and teach the students to develop their own plans and then act on them. The intentional process and repetition develop growth mindsets in both the students and educators.

Not every need or issue is approached the same way. Priorities must be set, finances may need to be secured, assignments made, timing projected, and preparations made. The school must identify what requires eventual action, immediate action, planning, and target dates. Use the following form to assist you.

Identify Issues Requiring Action, Issues You Need to Act on Immediately, Plans Needing Development, and Plans Needing Follow-through and Dates

Issues Requiring Action	Plans Needing Development
Immediate Issues to Act on by Dates	**Plans to Follow Through on by Dates**

There are a few orphans at Boys Town, Nebraska, a nonprofit organization that works with young people other schools in the United States had trouble dealing with, or who were in trouble, or whose parents or courts requested admission to best help the young.

In my first counselor position, I worked with a small number of students who lived in Boys Town satellite homes while attending Cathedral High School in Omaha, Nebraska. I did not know his whole background, but one student, Pete, said his parents moved often and never put him in school. When he was seven or eight, he saw another child reading and thought, *That's cool*. After that, he asked his parents if he could go to school.

Reading opens worlds of opportunities. Most of us take opportunities and blessings for granted. Students sitting in class but not trying to learn need to be made aware of a world full of opportunities available to the prepared. They need to be led and not wander around. Knowing about and having places they can fit initiates goal setting, planning, and moving forward to make life easier, financially secure, and happier. Ignorance and wandering through meaningless jobs make it hard. They need to implement Flow #3: Act, Plan, Act to become more informed.

Planning for academic and employment futures follows general guidelines with nuances crafted to individuals. Signing up for next year's courses is a similar process in the beginning, and it is individualized for each student. Selecting future careers consists of many similar steps taken to eventually arrive on a unique path to achieve job and career satisfaction in a world full of possibilities.

As a counselor, I understand the theory of not knowing or committing to a life plan too early. That makes sense, but it is a fallacy that students do not need to search for the right path because inspiration is destined to arrive on its own at the perfect time. That inspirational bird may never land on their doorstep, or they may not be paying attention when the best thing in life lands, then flies away. Students need to be offered early exposure to how to research and stay aware. Depending on chance is not an intelligent plan.

I am not in favor of the system used in some European countries that requires students in middle school to decide if they will go into the trades or pursue higher education. Many students are not sure of what they will do next week.

Discovering which careers and future schools are best is an outcome helped by practicing searching. In high school, practicing many searches with nothing to lose is easy, safe, and saves a lot of money by eliminating the first couple of wrong career, major, or schooling guesses.

If your high school does not prepare students through exploration, it must step up. Students need to know what to do before it is time so they are prepared to act ahead of time and then on time. Many will feel a change of majors or schools is necessary later in life. That is not a failure if they know how to adapt and succeed. Part of my book *Challenging College* dealt with what to do if you need to transfer or plan it.

Kevin, a former student, sent me a nice letter saying he remembered me talking about how to prepare to transfer. At that time, he was positive

> Students need to know what to do before it is time so they are prepared to act ahead of time and then on time.

it would never happen to him, yet transferring became his best path. Always be prepared.

Brent was a classmate of mine in our sophomore year at Creighton University. He wanted to experience the US, so he took his first year on the East Coast, his second in the Midwest, then finished in Oregon. Great planning.

Fortunately, I worked at schools that pushed for career success. My longest run was at Archbishop Bergan Catholic Schools in Fremont, Nebraska. This was not a private school for the rich. Most of the students were from blue-collar families, and the parish picked up half or more of the cost of their education. Hundreds of people helped with fundraisers every year. I worked at many big ones to help pay my own salary. That is real.

At Bergan, I gained ready access to students because a parish priest taught junior and senior theology. Since they worked weekends, their course met four days per week. The off day was mine for junior and senior career courses. We developed expectations that dropping out of school was not a consideration and continuing education beyond high school was.

Almost every year, 100 percent of the graduates went on to further their education. It was the expectation of the school, students, and parents. When students see that their peers are planning to stay in and go on to school, they stick with the crowd. When it becomes the group's expectation, you are more than halfway home.

You may be thinking, *He does not get it. That school is a fairy tale. It is not that way in my school.* The students at Bergan were not in a bubble. For most of my stint, there was no feeder, religious elementary school. The students came from eight public elementary schools with transfers from many middle and high schools and small towns. When they walked in the door, they walked into the expectation that they would graduate and continue their education. That was the deal. Continuing in school was backed by their own research for the best future for themselves. Success came because they worked at it, not because they were rich students with means. Almost all of those going to college had to apply for financial aid.

Eventually, the school board agreed to make my junior and senior careers courses one credit each and graduation requirements. It showed career preparation was serious business and that all the assignments were important. One was a five-page paper about what careers and schools the student was favoring. Parents had to read and sign it.

Some learned a valuable counterpoint that what is done in a career is not what they expected. Waiting to discover this when they are in post-secondary school, spending money, losing time, and considering dropping out is not a good plan. Skipping wrong choices may be key to earning a degree.

Action is needed to carry out good plans, or they may be a waste of time. Everyone wants a great future. Many need assistance to get there. Lay the facts out to groups to save time. Professionals know what to do and want to do it.

It might be assumed that potential dropouts know about their alternatives. That is a false assumption. If they really knew the consequences of dropping out instead of graduating, many would never do it. Never assume young people in fragile academic conditions know what they are doing to themselves. If they really did, many would pick up the pace.

FLOW #4: ASSESS, ADJUST, ADVANCE

Assuming artificial intelligence is not directing our trip, we must assess our current position to see where we are. We may need to adjust to keep going in the proper direction to advance with confidence to our destination. We have all done it and will continue the process. We must assess, adjust, and advance in most aspects of living or find we are doing the wrong things for the wrong reasons or in the wrong ways.

Do students self-assess and adjust to advance? They do if they are considering going out with someone or trying to make a team. How about preparing for their bigger future? That is more important than figuring out what to do this weekend.

Process builds a school system, its educators, and its students. Within this large context, we execute our personal processes and plans together. Consider these processes as flows to help those within and around your school:

1. Ease, Don't Squeeze
2. Mover Maps, Not Mud Maps
3. Act, Plan, Act
4. Assess, Adjust, Advance

The role of educators is to open minds to experiences and process the best. Any mind can wallow in the lowest levels of muddy thought and existence. Elevated mindsets capture the best the world has to offer and set out for more. In a great school, everyone shares in the accomplishments of others. Greatness is a shared mindset. It is how our mindsets roll.

It is important to periodically assess what is being done and adjust to advance to stronger positions. This can be done at the end of a program cycle or activity or mid-stream to make sure a program or effort is on course. Use the following form to identify what needs assessment and adjustment, what needs to advance, and which are priorities.

Identify Areas That Need Assessment or Adjustment, to Advance, or Are Priorities

Areas That Need Assessment	Areas That Need Adjustment
Areas That Need to Advance	**Areas That Are Priorities**

THINGS TO REMEMBER AND APPLY

○ We call it a mindset, but the mind is never set. It is a set of many things. Educators guide minds in positive directions. Helping to clear up known or unknown muddy thinking requires common sense and craft. Ease people toward wanting to grow.

○ Detach from the stress of work. Model this for students who must see they are not their problems. People live with, not within, problems. The more we practice a success process, the more it becomes routine. Routines become easier, automatic, and authentic parts of the way we live.

○ Young people want help. They may not know what they need or where and when they need it. It is our role to elevate students above restrictive options. Students want great advice. They want to be movers, not "mudders."

○ If schools believe in their mission statements and objectives, they should systematize the implementation of school-wide academic and social-emotional skill development to build student mindsets.

○ Plans help students find their best future. Educators teach students how to fulfill themselves and find their way. We must help students create potential career maps to guide them into their best future, or many will flounder in muddy ones.

○ Do not assume potential dropouts know their alternatives. If they knew the consequences of dropping out, many would not so it. Educators construct plans to help students. They model the process and teach students to develop their plans and then act on them.

o   Finding out that what is done in a career is not what was expected helps to avoid a wrong choice, and may prevent the student from leaving education. If your school does not prepare students through career and school exploration, it needs a boost. Students need to know what to do before it is time to choose, then be prepared to act ahead of time and then on time.

CHAPTER 6

PREVENTING SUICIDES AND DROPOUTS

It isn't what people think which is important,
but the reason they think what they think.
— EUGENE IONESCO

Disclaimer: The following chapter is not presented as a full suicide prevention or training program. This is an effort to set up a highly effective large-group presentation to prevent suicides. It is easy to do and can be a game-changer in the minds of many who witness it. If you encounter individuals considering suicide, promptly notify appropriate school officials and, per school policy, seek the assistance of trained professionals and follow their advice.

Anyone considering suicide needs to have a mindset adjustment at the highest, most important level. Life is too valuable to forfeit for any reason. Help in handling diffi-culties is available, and many are willing to provide it.

No one can have everything, but everyone should have a chance to have what is important, like graduating with a plan to be successful. Graduating has benefits and prereq-uisites — one of which is being alive. The goal and process of a great mindset is to keep the mind moving toward wins and not stuck in the mud of fear, hardship, worry, or loss, which may set the stage for considering suicide.

ESTABLISH THAT YOU CARE

It is important to establish that those attending a group presentation are cared for by you and others. They are not the situation they find themselves in. Thoughts of suicide may be experienced in passing or be more serious and need addressing. Does the person feel alone with no way out? That can be addressed.

When talking to individuals or in the preamble to the group presentation, I may use the same scenario I cov-ered with seniors before they went to college. I told them to imagine the largest university in the state with hun-dreds of thousands of graduates. At a large university, it is almost impossible for a student to be caught in a bad situation that has not been fixed before. The seniors offered suggestions of every pos-sible thing that could go wrong in college. I would list them on a

> At a large university, it is almost impossible for a student to be caught in a bad situation that has not been fixed before.

markerboard or screen and then cover potential solutions for each situation.

Here, again, is teaching without teaching. Some of the problems the group anticipated experiencing in college, like money or relationship difficulties, may be happening in the lives of some high school seniors. We covered potential solutions the students can put into motion in their college future or even that night.

Everyone can handle a few problems. That is life. It is when several pile on that people think about dropping out of college. Pertinent to this chapter, a pile of problems may muddy thoughts and cause them to consider dropping out of life.

Follow the advice offered in the *Ease Don't Squeeze* section of Chapter 5, and stay calm and composed as you take any talk of suicide seriously. Stay calm and relate that resources are available to help them find perspective and solutions to problems that many other students have found useful.

If a staff member hears anything from a student about suicidal thoughts, they cannot agree to keep silent. They must tell the student that they are required to confidentially get this information to the people trained to help and handle it. Schools have a plan in place with procedures, roles, and resources, such as calling 988, to assist with emergencies and suicides.

The chance of experiencing the suicide nightmare experienced by families, friends, and schools can be reduced by preventive action, such as the presentation further introduced in this chapter. Our goal is for you to never have to go one-on-one with a suicide crisis again.

BAD YEAR, GREAT LIFE

As a result of reading this chapter plus the download and free use of my presentation *Bad Year, Great Life*, suicide should be less of an issue in your school. Let me share a reference point.

Dr. John P. Dudley, a national school crisis consultant, was called into Columbine High School in Colorado to manage the heartache that followed their tragic mass school shooting in 1999. Dr. Dudley made it a policy to not endorse other people's books because he knew he would have been inundated with requests, but I will share a remark he made to me. It is not an endorsement of all my work, which Dr. Dudley has not reviewed.

Decades ago, I was at one of Dr. Dudley's crisis management workshops at Educational Service Unit #2 in Fremont, Nebraska. At the time, I had accumulated a few dozen presentations with no plan to publish them. Working full time in a middle and high school and part time with a university left me no extra time.

I gave an old, less-developed copy of *Bad Year, Great Life* to Dr. Dudley and asked him to please use it to save lives. Later, at a follow-up workshop, he approached me and said he had used it in a talk he gave to the student body at a large high school in Lincoln, Nebraska. Dr. Dudley added, "Afterward, the only thing they wanted to talk to me about was your presentation." He gave me a pat on the shoulder and moved on to help others.

You can go to neilfeser.com to get the free download of *Bad Year, Great Life*. The current version is better than the one I shared with Dr. Dudley, but the premise and execution remain simple. The visual impact and change in fragile mindsets are staggering, and I am giving it to you.

All educators want to prevent suicides but may not have the time to talk to everyone individually or have an effective group presentation that takes only eight minutes. Go for it. Several students in the group will have their mind mud cleared up. Others will remember it when they encounter severe doubts later in life. Help prevent a disaster now and later.

BAD YEAR, GREAT LIFE

Businesses give away samples to entice clients to buy their best. Is giving away the most visually and often emotionally impactful presentation in the *Skills Through Presentations* program a bad or good business decision? The answer: It is the right thing to do.

The visual impact is so strong that you will see shoulders in the crowd relax and smiles appear. I have had parents tell me their child came home and talked about what they learned. *Bad Year, Great Life* will help students in schools that purchase the program, and the message will spread to impact those who didn't experience the program firsthand. It does not get any better than that.

DROPOUTS DROP DOLLARS

Everyone, including potential dropouts, knows high school graduates earn more than dropouts. But do you know how much more it is:

- Over the person's lifetime?
- Per year of work?
- For each year invested in high school?
- Per hour of attendance in four years of high school?

You are about to learn facts that will make all the difference in the world to many facing the decision to drop out. Students seldom think in terms of getting paid to be in class and do homework. How much could they earn by staying in class and graduating? About $70 per hour for all hours spent in high school and at least an hour of studying per day outside of the classroom. Dropouts are not paid extra for their time spent in high school and studying.

Talk about changing a muddy mindset. It opens their eyes when potential dropouts see that most of the people sitting around them and doing the same work are, in effect, being paid $70 an hour because they are determined to graduate. That's $1.17 per minute they are paid — even for walking the halls and eating lunch. It is nice work that all of them can get if they go after it.

Your attention to this will also affect many mindsets of students who are not going to drop out but who are not fully applying themselves. The goal is not

> Students seldom think in terms of getting paid to be in class and do homework. How much could they earn by staying in class and graduating? About $70 per hour for all hours spent in high school and at least an hour of studying per day outside of the classroom. Dropouts are not paid extra for their time spent in high school and studying.

to get the average bonus from graduating from high school but to be in the upper half of better jobs, which might raise the "high school graduation bonus" earnings to $80 per hour. In the next section, you will find where to access the free presentation *Dropouts Drop Dollars*, which offers more presentation details to assist you.

PREVENTING THE MANY FORMS OF DROPPING OUT

Serving today's students does not merely seem to be more complicated — it *actually is*. Growing mixtures of abilities, backgrounds, and attitudes are a lot to handle, even with great circumstances and resources. Schools need to simplify something so that students, or a segment of students, are not fighting against being educated.

Unfortunately, students are only in middle school and high school once (or in some cases, twice, if they return). In this period of their lives, they either launch their drive to become something or miss great opportunities.

Teachers spend an inordinate amount of time dealing with students who are struggling because they are not giving their best efforts. They need a reason to try and consistently work. Money should not be the only mindset motivator, but when mindsets are weak, use it. Baby steps before big steps.

Educators need to help these students see through the muddy thinking of over- or under-confidence and a lack of practical insight. These are not hard to address, but it must be done effectively. Until students actively seek what education has to offer, the measure of success does not move up.

How do we help that to happen? What is available to make it happen? How can we get teachers to use what is available or obtain what they need to make it happen? How do we approach students and get them to take education seriously? At the extreme, how do we practically help anyone facing the decision to drop out and away from education and the ability to better self-determine their future? This can only happen in the brief window of teen years. This is not a time to be philosophical, political, trendy, or cuddly. What is real? Money is real. It is particularly real to students.

It might be posed that dropping out of high school is the stupidest financial decision a person can make. It may be the most unfulfilling decision. It may be the worst decision for the dropout's family and descendants. In Chapter 4, I alluded to a different perspective. In a sense, a person's present self is "married" to their future self. Marriage brings a sense of relying on a partner and doing what is best for them. Dropping out is not what is best for a partner. A future person should not have to pay a price for the misguided mistakes of the present self. It is too high a cost to pay.

I've included a synopsis of the *Dropouts Drop Dollars* presentation here, but you will be able to download the complete

> In a sense, a person's present self is "married" to their future self. Marriage brings a sense of relying on a partner and doing what is best for them. Dropping out is not what is best for a partner. A future person should not have to pay a price for the misguided mistakes of the present self.

presentation, which has all the math and options for how a counselor, math teacher, or other educator can present it using simple arithmetic to get the monetary points across. I am confident you will want to pursue it further. Included are several ways to enhance the message.

One case of a young person not graduating is one too many. It is hard to fathom why anyone does not want to graduate from high school, especially since most who do not graduate are capable of accomplishing it. Muddy mindsets are to blame. Real and unreal reasons must be sought out and defeated.

In one sense, not graduating is almost self-abuse. Why do that to one's future? It may even lead to child abuse or neglect when money is short and tempers flare.

Do not worry about not having enough people to do low-end jobs. There are too many people in the world who live in poor conditions and need to begin somewhere. Additionally, artificial intelligence will eventually make many low-end jobs unnecessary. If artificial intelligence can land a plane, it can fry hamburgers or wash dishes.

No one wants to be in low-end jobs when better alternatives are within reach for almost anyone with the proper help. It is easier to advance than it ever has been. There is so much help available. Opportunities abound for those who want to take advantage of them.

Certain students stay in high school but drop away from showing their best. They do not realize that they will soon be selling themselves as a product to future employers, spouses, children, and communities. Are they their best or cheap knockoffs of their potential? How can we help them raise their game?

We must develop the "want" in students. People who want something better adjust their mindsets to go after it. Educators can change attitudes. Potential dropouts can become stand-ups, rise-ups, risen-ups, and stay-ups. They can become people who do not waste time considering or planning not to be impactful people for themselves and their future families and communities.

We must develop the "want" in students. People who want something better adjust their mindsets to go after it. Educators can change attitudes. Potential dropouts can become stand-ups, rise-ups, risen-ups, and stay-ups.

DROPOUTS DROP DOLLARS

Dropouts Drop Dollars from the *Skills Through Presentations* program hits home in terms the young understand: Money in their pockets. All math and financial concepts are ready through the free download at neilfeser.com.

What about college earnings? For years, I used the *Skills Through Presentations* effective presentation Shredding Money to encourage students to continue their education after high school. Anything less than 100 percent post-high-school training made me evaluate how I could do better. All can grow.

REDUCE PHYSICAL, FINANCIAL, AND EMOTIONAL SUICIDE

People do not consider physical, financial, or emotional suicide if they see that things can eventually change and are going to change for the better. Suicide is a last-ditch effort to get away from the real or imagined pain they are experiencing.

Imagined pain resulting from an over-active imagination is a tainted misunderstanding, extrapolation, or interpretation of reality. Yet, it appears real for the person wrapped up in it. It is important to help the suffering person identify the true situation so that it can be addressed with help.

INCENTIVE DISCOUNTS

Saving lives and potential careers by preventing dropouts are two of my priorities. Strengthening emotional perspectives through the *Skills Through Presentations* supports the prevention of suicide and addresses many aspects of growth.

In addition to providing the presentations to all schools for free, if a school presents *Bad Year, Great Life* and *Dropouts Drop Dollars* to the student body in an assembly, the *Skills Through Presentations* program may be purchased at a reduced price. Details are at neilfeser.com.

Schools can also add the Booster Discount if a benefactor, business, booster, or booster group pays for the *Skills Through Presentations* program. Invite possible payers to the assembly where you deliver the two presentations. They will be impressed by your efforts to help students and the students' reactions. Supporters will feel great about helping hundreds or thousands of students. People and organizations want to help. Share growth, ownership, and credit.

There is also a Booster Un-Discount available. If the booster waves their discount, I will donate the full *Skills Through Presentations* program to a needy school in Africa. Helping future generations there is a way of paying reparations to people whose past generations suffered. In this scenario, the booster will be sent the school's name and be given credit. More details can be found at neilfeser.com.

THINGS TO REMEMBER AND APPLY

o   Take talk of suicide seriously. Anyone considering suicide needs a mindset adjustment at the highest level.
Life is too valuable to forfeit for bad reasons. Stay calm
and relate that resources are available to help find perspective and solutions to problems in ways many other
students have found useful.

o   All educators want to prevent suicides. A group presentation that takes only eight minutes is highly effective. Go for it. Several students will have their mind
mud cleared up.

o   Potential dropouts may engage when they discover that
people sitting around them and doing the same work
are, in effect, being paid $70 an hour to be there be-
cause they are determined to graduate.

o   Educators help students see through the muddy thinking resulting from over- or under-confidence and a lack
of practical insight. Until students seek what education
has to offer, the measure of success does not rise.

o   Dropping out of high school may be the stupidest financial decision a person can make — and the most unfulfilling. One case of not graduating is one too many.
Muddy mindsets are to blame. Real and unreal reasons
must be sought and defeated.

o   Students will sell themselves as a product to future employers, spouses, children, and communities. Are they
their best or cheap knockoffs?

CHAPTER 7

BUILD STRENGTHS, ATTACK WEAKNESSES

I tell people: If you don't want to get into positive thinking,
that's O.K. Just eliminate all the negative thoughts
from your mind, and what is left will be fine.
— BOB ROTELLA

In the last chapter, I addressed saving lives and aiming to graduate. Those who commit to these goals are now in an interesting position. Aldous Huxley said, "Every ceiling, when reached, becomes a floor upon which one walks as a matter of course and prescriptive right." Once an accomplishment is achieved, there is more to do, steps to take, and levels to attain en route to the highest level possible.

Humans take things for granted. The Christmas gifts that once were so exciting are now stored in a closet.

Coveted awards are memories. No high school student wants to re-achieve grade school goals. We need to keep raising our games and working to meet the new challenges we set and those that find us.

Beyond needless worries, demands of others, and challenges from everywhere, we must elevate our skills to better position ourselves to help those in need. Students may not be getting enough help from home or their environment to handle problems. Even great parents get snowed under by multiple responsibilities and needs of their children. In Chapter 4, I reviewed many areas of need and school opportunities. Society leans on its educators to fill the gaps, and educators want to step up. At times, they need the tools that demonstrate that prevention saves time in the long run.

How often do teachers wish their students were totally into the concept they are teaching? How often do student minds wander because they do not see the topic's relevance? All teachers and students have experienced this. We appreciate and respect teachers who adapt to draw in the students without watering down their message.

Professional educators do not need more statistics from local, state, or national surveys that show students do not think they need to spend time on things they feel they will never need. We were all like that when we were students. No one wants their time wasted. People will buy in if they see their time invested.

We all know people who may love one subject and hate another, while

> No one wants their time wasted. People will buy in if they see their time invested.

others in a class feel the opposite. There may be five or more clock-watchers in any classroom who wish they were anywhere else. What should the teacher do? How do we help teachers help students elevate their vision and want to go into their classrooms and learn? The "why" behind paying attention to a topic is important. It may be more important when it is not addressed. Schools need to adequately address how and why courses are taught.

MAKE TIME TO GAIN ATTENTION AND TIME BACK

The fact that students need to understand *why* they are taking courses is often overlooked. The staff may think it is obvious, but students frequently do not know why a graduation or pre-requisite requirement exists. Knowing why may create a difference in attitude. They may not like the logic or reasons, but at least they will know why they are there. Simply taking the time to explain the importance of a course may save conferences with students who do not want to be there because they have never been exposed to its relevance. Much more on developing this theme will be covered in Chapter 9.

If a teacher sits back and thinks their students must come to them to pass the requirement, that is problematic and not a professional position. If a course is required for a reason, it is important. The teacher should establish the reasoning for the course to help students want to learn the material because of its importance. Students should not merely aim for passing. Instead, they should focus on accomplishing greatness in an important course. If a teacher cannot sell the importance of a course, that is a problem.

Students are better consumers than they used to be. Sell them your course.

Not everything has to be fun and engaging. Students know they are supposed to pay attention, but 40–50 minutes is a long time if nothing piques their interest. If an education professional never teaches outside the lines to draw students closer to enjoying the subject matter, students will not try to find their own way to it.

Gain or regain the skill, acquire the means, and show relevance where it never existed or was lost. It can be done. It must be done. Before returning to what the school and teachers can do to build the relevance and success of subjects, let's be reminded that, in general, the top half of students only need advice. It is the bottom half that needs advice, encouragement, *and* motivational support. They will be fine if they figure life out, no matter how tough they act. Many are unsure, or they would not be making the decisions that they are.

FRAGILE MINDSETS

It is important for the young to feel accepted for who they are, even if they do not know who they are. Welcome to ongoing middle school. Students need to be given permission to be confused and the encouragement to gradually put themselves and their minds together. They will be okay. Encourage them to hang in there. All adults went through what they are experiencing, and most of us came out fine. Be patient.

The young want to look good all the time. They think they need to be great in someone else's eyes if not their own. This perspective is not all bad. The young need to strive to be better, but not at everything.

It takes time to become an adult. Brain development continues until the mid-20s, perhaps longer. It takes time for an adult to form. No one fully knows who they are in grade school, middle school, or even high school. It is the role of educators to help youth through the process of maturing and support them as they grow. All young people want and need familial, relational, educational, and community support. It takes a village to raise a child, and the village includes the school. No school represents the village. It has its place as a state of helpfulness.

> It takes time for an adult to form. No one fully knows who they are in grade school, middle school, or even high school. It is the role of educators to help youth through the process of maturing and support them as they grow.

We need to be the fire that works to protect the identities of children and build respect for all. This means leaving no one out, and most importantly, it includes our bodies, minds, and spirits.

Everyone wants to be treated with respect. All deserve it. Of that mindset, I am sure.

TRY ON LIFE TO SEE WHAT FITS

A person's youth is a time of trying on life to see what fits. It is sad when someone never even tries to do the things they might eventually be the best at. Why stand in that mud?

A parallel is found in choosing a career. If a person only knows about five or six careers, they'll have a hard time finding two good choices, let alone the most fulfilling one. Looking into 20–30 career options improves the odds of having 10 good choices and several great ones. Youth is a time of safe explorations — both brief and in-depth.

The *Occupational Outlook Handbook* is free online and is updated regularly to give great information on hundreds of careers and fields.[11] It can be found any-time. If students finish their work early and have internet access, they could spend time learning about careers. The teacher can ask random students to share what they learned before class ends. Anyone with an upgraded career mindset and internet access, including parents, can use it.

When the opportunity arises, the teacher may refer-ence where the subject or field being taught is used in the careers discussed. Never pass up an opportunity to make the subject matter more relevant to those in the room who need reasons to pay attention.

We reach happiness by taking diverse routes to great-ness, not languishing in weaknesses because we fear we might not look good trying. Those who avoid trying limit their possibilities of success. We want to help the young prepare for the future. To do that, we must teach them to laugh at themselves if they screw up. The best way to teach that is to model it.

These days, almost no one has experienced climb-ing back up onto a horse after being thrown off. In older times in the Americas, there were cowboys and cowgirls of many races who would capture and "break" wild horses by climbing on and holding on for dear life while the horse tried to buck them off. It was hard work made harder by landing on hard ground. It took a tough mindset and a tough body to be a cowboy or cowgirl.

Many indigenous tribes in the Americas took a different approach. They would lead the horse into a pond and slide on. It was more difficult for the horse to buck in the water, and if the rider was thrown off, the landing was much softer. The indigenous tribes were also very tough, but they had a more thoughtful mindset and approach.

Today's youth may shy away from attempting difficult things because they do not want to fail or fall. If we can teach them nothing else, we must teach them that it is okay and necessary to fail as a prerequisite to becoming successful. Greatness is never attained through a fear of failure. Greatness comes from challenging failure.

THE WAY OF THE INTELLIGENT MINDSET

Many young people might hesitate to get on a wild horse and get thrown off onto hard ground. But they might line up to try to ride a wild horse and get thrown into the water. Some would pay to try. Follow the way of the intelligent mindset. The right mentality powered by practice, persistence, and patience with the self is required to develop bravery.

Follow the way of the intelligent mindset. The right mentality powered by practice, persistence, and patience with the self is required to develop bravery.

In modern times, no one tries to climb rock walls without a safety rope. It makes sense, but have we lost our edge? When I was young, we climbed in trees and barn rafters, and behind the school at recess we scaled walls made of large natural rocks that were cemented together. We never used safety ropes. They were probably there, but I do not remember any playground supervisors. We paid no attention. We were too busy taking turns climbing.

As an adult, I went back to look at those 15-foot-high rock walls to find they were only eight feet high at most. I was disappointed but realized we were little boys with no mountains in sight. It is the principle of the thing.

Live by principles but acknowledge that, at times, the truth is annoying. I never returned to the walls again and want to remember them as being 15 feet high. At times, it is better to lose a very unimportant truth than one's edge. Being a little bigger than reality is part of a great, confident mindset. In my mind, the walls are now 20 feet high.

Life requires much more than physical bravery, which may be the easiest kind. Parents will ignore any physical danger to protect their children. If people have choices, it is harder to be brave. How do we get youth to take on challenges and deal with them? A typical, difficult problem to deal with in school is the bully mindset. Fortunately, this mindset can be reset, along with the mindsets of victims and bystanders.

TRANSITIONING BULLIES INTO BUILDERS

Every school deals with bullying. In *Skills Through Presentations,* a different approach does not try to break bullies like wild horses by riding them until they submit. They are guided into the water, where they are seen by victims and bystanders as less threatening or effective. Eventually, they, too, see the light, grow up, and find that they can make more friends by attracting them than berating them. Unique approaches reveal that bullies and leaders share similar skills but work in different directions. Bullies need direction. It is rewarding to see bullies transition into builders.

In Chapter 3, I touched on slavery, both ancient and current. Too many give into the "slavery" of illicit drugs, crime, or taking advantage of others to compensate for their perceived poor lot. Those weak, defeatist ways of life result from and continue muddy thinking. No one must give up their power.

It is a poor choice to give in to the form of slavery led by bullies. Children affected by current bullying have no idea about the hardships of living in slavery. Slave owners and segregationists were just common bullies with the local law on their side. The same is true of tyrants of all kinds, including those who abuse in families.

School bullies do not have chains; they only have weak sentences. Victims and bystanders only *think* they are strong — until they do not. Every day, victims learn to throw off

School bullies do not have chains; they only have weak sentences. Victims and bystanders only *think* they are strong — until they do not.

weak mindsets and discover that it is easier to stand up to bullies who act overly important. Students may be naturally strong. Others need to be led. Lead them.

THINGS TO REMEMBER AND APPLY

o Beyond needless worries, demands of others, and challenges from everywhere, we must elevate our skills to help those in need.

o How do we help teachers help students elevate their visions and want to learn? The staff may think it is obvious, but students often do not know why a graduation or pre-requisite requirement exists. Knowing the rationale may create a difference in attitude.

o Students should aim for greatness in any important course. If a teacher cannot sell its importance, there is a problem. Sell it.

o If a person only knows about five careers, finding two good choices is hard. Looking into many careers improves the odds of having good choices.

o Youth may shy away from attempting difficult things because they do not want to fail or fall. We must teach them it is okay and necessary to fail as a prerequisite to becoming successful. Teach students to laugh at themselves if they screw up. The best way to teach this is to model it.

o A typical, difficult problem to deal with in school is the bully mindset. It can be reset, along with the mindsets of victims and bystanders. Every day, victims learn to throw off weak mindsets and discover it is easier to stand up to bullies who act overly important. Students may be naturally strong. Others need to be led. Lead them.

CHAPTER 8

ROUT DOUBT IN SCHOOL ENVIRONMENTS

I'll be more enthusiastic about encouraging thinking outside the box when there's evidence of any thinking going on inside it.
— **TERRY PRATCHETT**

Note: *This chapter is more for administrators than other educators, but all will learn from it, especially in matters of role Perspective. In a review and upgrade of my school's programs, I worked with a superintendent-consultant from suburban Chicago. At the end of the week, he told me, "You are a counselor who thinks like an administrator." Was that an insult?*

True, I have overseen dozens (and dozens) of school programs, and I know that thinking must adjust to the role. The person in charge of school maintenance should not have the same thoughts as the people cleaning the rooms. I think Heads of Maintenance are among the smartest people in schools. They exemplify a no-nonsense mindset and get the job done right the first time. In a school, everyone is in the maintenance department. Some work with objects. Some work with minds. Let's dig deeper.

There are two types of student attendance. The first is physically being in school and focused, and the second is mental attentiveness. The first is obvious; the second is nebulose. Eyes may be looking forward but not at the teacher's content topic. We will address how to sell academic subjects to very reluctant buyers, the uninterested students, in Chapter 9.

Many Christians believe in purgatory, either as a place or state, where souls go after death to be cleansed before going to heaven, an advanced state of purity. I have it on good authority that all time spent in faculty meetings and in-services counts as double time off any stay in purgatory.

And you thought you were wasting time.

Sitting or standing in the same spot and following a dry agenda may be considered an efficient means of delivery or a rut of muddy, lost attention, even to people who want to be in the know. Everything works well for part of a meeting until it doesn't work for the whole meeting or every other meeting.

What if faculty were asked to attend either a faculty meeting or a funeral? The choice is between donuts and ham casserole. If faculty meetings bring out that same level of excitement as a funeral, administrators can address the concern by dusting off techniques used when they were teachers. Administrators know many teaching styles. They know about proximity to off-topic students. They may need to get out of their chairs and navigate around teachers who are doing crossword puzzles in meetings.

The alternative to invigorating faculty meetings is kissing attention goodbye along with the enthusiasm needed to support agenda topics. The same is true of classrooms.

Imagine going to six faculty meetings a day, every day. That is what school is like for some students. The level of excitement and glee many faculty bring to faculty meetings parallels the energy students may bring into classrooms. Administrators must reset their mindsets by firing up faculty for meetings, just as teachers must ignite the mindsets of students for class. It does not make any difference if people are expected to have great attitudes. Attitudes must be elevated and reinforced to make participation infectious. No coach starts his classes the same way he does his pre-game speech. Not even close.

> Imagine going to six faculty meetings a day, every day. That is what school is like for some students.

DOUBT KILLS PROGRAMS, MORALE, SPIRIT, AND SUCCESS

One school I worked in planned to introduce a new drug prevention program that involved students coming forward to let an adult know if one of their friends was getting too far into drug or alcohol use. No punishments were involved. No public or faculty-wide disclosures were planned. The only goal was interventions to keep students safe in a confidential way. There were questions, but no serious dissenting remarks were made at the faculty meeting, where the proposal was explained before it was introduced at an all-school assembly.

When the day came to present the programs, the students were not receptive, neutral, or willing to listen. The presenters were surprised to find students totally up in arms and closed-minded. Apparently, one or more teachers must not have liked the program. They had not voiced their opinion at the meeting, but they had talked unfavorably about it with influential students. Information, misinformation, or disinformation spread fast.

The program had no chance. Many faculty and administrators took turns trying to reason with the student body, but the students had made up their minds. They would not rat on anyone and would not participate.

The probably too-idealistic program was dropped, along with any good it might have done. Even if the teachers who sabotaged the program were right, it was not their call to kill it before it had a chance.

Another situation in schools happens when a segment — or all — of the women feel they do not have an equal voice with men, either because of their numbers or the tendency of male administrators to favor male friends. You may substitute another category for women. That is a mindset powder keg that needs to be addressed.

Other factions and frictions can be created by unequal money distributed to departments or teams or schedules of sports that still ignore equality. There must be an avenue for staff to safely voice disappointment, distress, or dissent without feeling they may be reprimanded, have their loyalty questioned, or find themselves equal on the surface but unequal where it matters. It would take an additional book to address all the possibilities. Speak up to someone who cares.

Having worked with several principals with different styles of operating, I developed a policy of meeting privately with a new administrator early on to make one thing clear: Behind closed doors, I might strongly disagree with a policy, plan, or decision, but when I walked out the door, we were on the same page. I would support the topic, position, or policy. I may not be a cheerleader, but I would not bad-mouth it. Why?

Administratively and practically, a school cannot run if the staff and students see those in supervisory capacities moving in opposite directions. The policy, program, or plan will not work, the staff will become divided, and doubt about other things will increase.

As a quick ego check, I'll admit that, at times, my opinion turned out to be wrong, but the unified action of the administration and staff made the program work (emphasis on *unified*).

At other times, I was right, but the program would die on its own. This was never gratifying for me. No one wants to see time and resources wasted.

The best thing I could do when the next program was being considered that I did not see as workable was to prepare and present a more nuanced case. The administrative decision might be the same, but those in charge could consider my doubts and prepare a strategy to handle problems and any potential fallout. Any administration supported by yes-people is doomed. Long live the king who listens.

The difference between success and failure is being ready for the bumps any program taking on a worthy challenge will encounter. We can handle some problems. A tendency to have problems or difficulty solving recurring ones because of flaws in thinking or procedures must be avoided.

TRANSITIONING CRITICISMS INTO CORRECTIONS

Almost every staff has a lead critic who pokes holes in anything different from the way it has always been done. Mudslinging is part of that colleague's identity. Perhaps the person has no say-so at home, so they make up for it at work. This person develops allies. Their views cannot be ignored.

Actively listen to disagreement. Better to hear it in meetings than to have it fester in hallways. As stated before, to improve a program or situation, legitimate concerns should be considered before they become problems. Embracing criticism in the planning stages accelerates a program's success.

If an issue arises as a critic prophesied, and then the issue is fixed, the administrator should make it a point to thank the critic. They were right, and their initiative helped solve a problem. Everyone feels good. Win-win. The administrator should ask the critic to bring any concerns directly to them next time. This circumvents pockets of dissent in the ranks and gives the administrator a chance to make corrections or to counter the criticisms. In any event, the school is better prepared to advance.

The intelligent administrator can put a proposal out and ask the staff to shoot holes in it. This shows confidence in the staff and their wisdom. Many schools have staff working on administrative, counseling, or other degrees. They may have just learned cutting-edge information on the matter at hand. That input may be very important to the ultimate success of a program.

If the staff make good suggestions, pay out the credit. Never limit the scope of wins. Staff will support programs for which they feel ownership. Share the glory.

THE SAME PAGE MAY NOT BE THE RIGHT PAGE

Is it always good to have the same mindset? No. At least at the beginning, when not everyone thinks the same way in the planning stages. Unique perspectives often expose the diverse viewpoints of the audience the school wants to influence. When all start from the same spot in planning, the process may be truncated, making it possible to ignore unique or potential perspectives that will be encountered in the execution of the plan. Too late is not a great time to replan. Foresee the worst and prepare when steps can still be taken to help students maintain momentum.

It is important for all involved to unite in the execution of agreed-upon strategies and plans. When students observe the whole staff moving them in the direction of success, they hear a consistent message. Almost all students like at least someone on the staff, so they are more likely to accept the message.

> It is important for all involved to unite in the execution of agreed-upon strategies and plans. When students observe the whole staff moving them in the direction of success, they hear a consistent message.

Educators and student bodies do not tend to be negative people, but they do have biases toward their disciplines, beliefs, etc. They are human. Make the tent big enough for all and let them be heard in appropriate ways. Be fair, and most will work for the common good.

Some administrators will put something out for staff input after the decision has been made. That administrator has a set mindset and is overconfident about the direction the staff will go and, instead, only wants their blessing.

I attended one district meeting at which the staff of many schools sat at mixed tables and made recommendations on how to proceed in addressing a common problem. After sharing ideas, representatives of each table presented their results. All felt good about the input — except for the person in charge. The superintendent totally shot down the input because it went against what he had already decided.

Everyone felt betrayed. They had wasted their time. Even worse, their input was not seen as important. The disconnect may have occurred because those in charge of the agenda did not clearly explain their vision to the superintendent. More likely, they misunderstood that his goal was to substantiate a pre-ordained decision he thought all would agree was best.

Walk a mile in my mud. If asking for input from staff, students, parents, or the public, be ready to seriously consider it. Your reasons for not using their suggestions must hold up. Clear communication in every direction unites all involved. Not acknowledging that those in charge are considering input is interpreted as not caring. Let people know they were heard and then address why their proposal cannot work at this time. No snow jobs allowed. Reasoning holds up, or it does not. Choosing not to communicate never holds up. Instead, set up success through accurate agendas and plans. Elevate people to think and act above the mud. Then, you have made a difference.

One of my principals released me to attend a drug use prevention workshop to learn from national experts. We started out sharing ideas about what we thought was needed. That was fine, but topic after topic went on and on as they asked us what we thought. Hours later, the person in charge asked if we understood that their goal was not to present new research and programs but to collect ideas. Everyone around me said, "No," in unison. His expression did not change, but an extended pause confirmed that someone had dropped the ball.

Before seeking input from staff, students, or parents, clearly inform everyone about the purpose and plan of the meeting. Beyond being a courtesy, several people will put thought into the agenda if the topic is important to them. They will bring ideas and enthusiasm. Variety is the spice of mindsets. It may not be the idea people present that works, but one spurred by it.

> Variety is the spice of mindsets. It may not be the idea people present that works, but one spurred by it.

Not everyone has to work on every problem. There are enough problems to go around. Those who are not interested in one topic can use their time on something they are fired up about. Those with passion will more strongly share their cases with everyone who will be asked to work toward success.

The river of school success is made of the efforts of the human tributaries that join it. Large rivers are made from smaller rivers. One person is not your school. In your system, "we" are a school. I can educate, but *we* can educate better. Be sure everyone knows how important they are to the school and to you. This mindset flows top-down and bottom-up. From far-left to far-right. From outside to inside and back.

THINGS TO REMEMBER AND APPLY

- Heads of Maintenance are among the smartest people in schools. They exemplify a no-nonsense, clear-the-mud, get-the-job-right mindset. Everyone in schools maintains things, people, and minds.
- Administrators must set mindsets by firing up faculty for meetings, just as teachers must ignite the mindsets of students for class. Attitudes must be elevated and reinforced to make participation infectious.
- An avenue must exist for staff to offer disappointment, distress, or dissent without feeling reprimanded, have loyalty questioned, or find themselves "equal" but unequal where it matters.
- Actively listen to disagreement before it festers. Legitimate concerns should be considered before they are problems. Embracing criticism when planning accelerates a program's success. If an issue arises as a critic prophesied and then the issue is fixed, the administrator should make it a point to thank the critic. Their initiative helped solve a problem. Everyone feels good. Win-Win.
- Is it always good to have the same mindset? No. Everyone should not think the same way in the planning stages. Unique perspectives expose diverse viewpoints, which the school wants and needs to influence. The difference between success and failure is being ready for the bumps any program that is taking on a worthy challenge will encounter.
- Before seeking input from staff, students, or parents, clearly inform everyone about the purpose and plan of the meeting or proposal. If asking for input from staff, students, parents, or the public, be ready to seriously consider it.

CHAPTER 9

BE THE FIRE IN THE FURNACE, NOT THE FILTER

Strategic thinking is like showering. You have to keep doing it.
— OLAN HENDRIX

Movies have been made about leaders who stood up and turned a terrible school around. In Chapter 1, I explained how a person must be a little naïve to be an idealist or, often, to act. If people knew how hard it is to make massive change, they might not start. The key is for one person to get others to work together to pull off amazing things. It is not on me, but "we." Thomas Edison is heralded as a great inventor, but other people did most of the work required to fulfill his visions.

All people can be leaders in improving their schools. Keep it simple and under control. Leading is not accepting excuses and mediocre behavior or accomplishments from students who could ascend to where they deserve to be. When educators have the opportunity, they should not *act* like they are in charge — they must *be* in charge. Eddie Rickenbacker said, "Think things through, then follow through." Educators in a school are charged with executing real learning in a vibrant environment through working together.

Every school or school system has people who are the fire and those who succumb to being the filter. A group of teachers and administrators who are the fire get up early and go to school, ready to deal with anything that comes their way because students and their futures are very important to them.

The filters are teachers and administrators who let the students flow past them and through the school without being elevated. They are the few who fill slots, not seize opportunities to inspire. They may have had the fire early in their careers, but something reduced their flame. That does not mean it cannot be regained. It is not hard to sharpen a knife or a mindset. Education is all about learning and relearning for students and staff. Educators must continuously rekindle that fire in their social-emotional furnace. It takes an energetic mindset to lead students.

WORK TOWARD UPSIDES; PREPARE FOR DOWNSIDES

As a counselor, I worked hard to help people maximize positive mindsets and especially to help young women continue their education after high school. Why? Because some of them were, or will be, misled, let down, and punished because they believed in the young man they married. I knew I could not prevent abortions or abusive situations in future marriages, but I could help them to be prepared. They needed an education and career to help them make a living and take care of their children if the father did not. Almost all the women I worked with continued their education.

Not every year, but at times, because I could see a few individuals heading into trouble, I would have a session only with the senior women. The message was clear: Protect yourself, protect your mindset, protect your future children.

I told the young women to think twice before selecting a weak man to marry, thinking they would be able to change him. They should make it clear that he must first change himself to be worthy of the woman he says he loves. If he was not willing to do that, she should move on. There are many great men in the world waiting for a great woman who thinks highly of herself and wants to build a great marriage.

My message to men was simpler: Man up. If you want a great lady, be worthy of a great lady.

No two lives are equal, but as a thought experiment, assume they are. It is harder to live with a weak mindset than a strong one. As educators, we must mandate growth, strength, and positive mindsets. If a great mindset sinks in, it is a win. If it develops later, it can still be a win.

> No two lives are equal, but as a thought experiment, assume they are. It is harder to live with a weak mindset than a strong one.

People need to see themselves getting to where they want to go. Just like a pilot or sea captain may need a navigator, students sometimes need outsiders like teachers or others to check their progress and make sure they are going in a great direction. Outsiders or parents often challenge students.

Confirmation bias is seeing what we expect to see. No one drops out because they think school will really help them. Many low achievers in school do not see anything or enough in school that makes a difference for them, so they think, *What's the point*? The earlier we address this perception, the faster people can grow. Likewise, the earlier we build strengths, the faster people can channel them to address weaknesses and enlarge opportunities.

Desirability bias is seeing what we want to see. That can mean we are fooling ourselves, or we might turn it to mean we see a great, desirable future. We need to help youth get out of fictional desirability and into building reality-based success.

TO TEACH IT, FIRST SELL IT

We struggle to focus on what barely interests us. Teachers may not care for, and may even dislike, some subjects taught in other areas of the school, while the teachers in those rooms love what they teach. It is a free country — for the teachers, that is. Not so much for the students, who are often required to take courses or go through topics they may not like. They do not have to love or like what any teacher offers — that is their right — but it may not be good in practice. How can teachers help students with struggling attention?

Teachers must go more than halfway because struggling students are seldom willing to meet you in the middle until they see a good reason to do so. Teachers should never assume the reasons their subject or content is important are obvious. In the mindset of the reluctant student, the reasons are obviously not obvious.

It makes little difference what is in the teacher's notes if the student's mindset is not in the game. As previously mentioned, attention to the teacher's topic must be continuously and intentionally regained. In a room of students, often several are not with the teacher. As with administrators, teachers know many teaching theories or techniques to access attention and invigorate rooms. Is that enough?

We dance around what is missing from many underachieving mindsets. Knowing they must be in school and take courses is not enough to motivate students. The following questions are oversimplified or overlooked. To engage many students, they need answers to important questions like:

- Why am I in any, or many, courses?
- Why is all, or specific, course content important?
- When and where will this course or content be useful in my future?
- What difference will any of the content make in my life?
- Who makes money using this content?
- What does understanding this information lead to?

It is important for all students to know why they must learn the material in a course or what it can do for them. These could be important missing links. Adults usually know the reason they do what they do at work. Students also need to know. Without answers, there are holes in reasoning, commitment, motivation, and success.

As mentioned elsewhere, as a new counselor, I assumed students knew about a reasonable number of careers. Then, they demonstrated they could not name or define many at all. This is paralleled by students who lack understanding of the courses and the content.

It was often my responsibility to supervise the compilation of the registration handbook of courses for the coming school year. Course descriptions were all about the course content. This is important, but for the struggling mindset, it does not help explain why the course is important or where it can and will help the student. Being a prerequisite or qualifying course for college admission is an insufficient reason for the struggling mindset.

I spent decades working in front of real students to find out what works. My first read was simple. The reactions in their eyes immediately told me what was working and whether I should keep going or change the approach, information, or activity. Here is some advice for teachers: If you see a lack of enthusiasm, insert a reason why the content is important. Do it early. Do it often. Anticipate it. Have your rationale ammunition ready. In what careers, interactions, or problem-solving situations is it used? What are some important examples of its use? How can teachers best present reasons to be in courses that light up the students' eyes?

In the reign of certain administrations, it was always one of my favorite parts of a faculty meeting when the administrator set aside a few minutes for each department to share their interesting plans for the coming weeks. It builds morale when teachers get to tell their stories and helps them appreciate that great things are going on around them. They may be able to cross-teach, reinforce each other, and show students that school is a coordinated effort and the teachers are working together to support them.

Never pass up an opportunity to showcase that topics presented in multiple disciplines have multiple applications. Creativity and retention are increased by multi-layered, multi-discipline teaching and thinking. Building stronger, more versatile mindsets everywhere has a cascading effect.

> Creativity and retention are increased by multi-layered, multi-discipline teaching and thinking. Building stronger, more versatile mindsets everywhere has a cascading effect.

Once teachers are aware of what's being taught in different areas of the school, those in a single department should create their own sales campaign or work on a campaign together. What works in one course can work in others to sell the field. One teacher may have great reasons students should care about their subject that another teacher can use. Compile the whole campaign and share it with other departments. In faculty meetings or in-service days, show off your best.

First, prepare your reasons to establish great ways the field is important and ways it is used. List careers in which the field is important and what career or life skills are sharpened by the course or field. Next, do the same for courses. Finally, show why today's content is important in the same ways you did the program and courses. Use the following forms to help you establish your reasoning. Share with other educators, critique, and improve. Together, you will elevate your courses, departments, and school as mindsets advance and the mud of student doubt and confusion is washed away.

Downloadable copies of these forms are available in the expanded format along with more suggestions for departments in *Selling Your Curriculum,* a division of the *Skills Through Presentations* program.

Department or Field: _____

List reasons why this field is important and what it can do for students.

Why this field is important:	Ways this field is used in society:
Jobs using the field's information:	**Skills sharpened by this field:**

Course: _____

List reasons why this course is important and what it can do for students.

Why this course is important:	Ways content is used in society:
Jobs using course information:	**Skills sharpened by this course:**

Concept or Content: _____

List reasons why this concept or content is important and what it can do for students.

Why this content is important:	Ways content is used in society:
Jobs using this content:	**Skills sharpened by this content:**

The organized ideas above give you a structure and facts to substantiate the importance of your subject matter. Do not give all the information in one speech. Instead, spread it out in the first week or month of the semester to reinvigorate motivation and make sure all absentees hear the message.

Do not write your sales pitch using academic terminology to impress a professor. Write to students and possibly to parents. Even better, create a brief pitch to parents for a time like registration conferences.

Think of this effort to motivate as a sales presentation because that is what it is. Teaching is selling. Educators may want to think of it in loftier, academic, etheric terms, but teaching is getting the students to buy what educators are selling. Yes, it is that simple. Salesmen teach their customers *why* their product is great for them. Teachers must sell the worth of their content and concepts that are great for students.

Following up on the idea of having teachers and departments briefly share what they have coming up, try this exercise. To learn from each other, the faculty might have a contest and let teachers "sell" their courses to other teachers. All those present can offer their critiques and suggestions. Give prizes paid for by the administration for the best in categories of your choice.

It is possible that one vibrant teacher is great at this and can represent the department when talking to a larger group. I did a form of this when preparing students for the next year's registration. Half of what I said to individual students was the same material, so I covered that with the group and gained more time to do a better job with individual students — especially with students who needed extra time.

In Chapter 6, I spoke about how I had at or near 100 percent of my graduates going on to higher education. The way to make that happen is to sell the prospect of higher education so that little else makes much sense. There are thousands of books on salesmanship. There are no books on how to get people to be bored with what you offer.

Polish the explanation or demonstration of why the content of the course is — or will eventually be — important to the students. Once they buy in, their grades, teaching skills, and everyone's overall success will synergistically grow. Swinging five more students to enjoy the class can upgrade the atmosphere and enthusiasm. Five can become seven because others will join the movement when they see students enjoying the content. Increasing the wins equals fewer conferences and make-up work. Changing low-end mindsets changes lives.

It is essential that the disengaged be thrown a lifeline. Do not expect them to do cartwheels; expect them to participate more and to be more. Set the bar for yourself and them. By elevating your energy about your work, where it can be used in society, employment, and enjoyment of life or in helping others, can make a huge difference in student application of effort and enjoyment of your course and its content.

Chapter 2 details a leadership exercise in which the leader moves forward with a big rubber band hooked to the finger of the follower. The follower sees the leader taking the lead and must pick up their pace to follow.

Before a race, a starter may raise a flag or a pistol to signal the beginning of the race. I was the starter for cross-country meets for decades. I told the runners exactly what I was going to do, then did exactly what I said. I held up, then blew, a whistle. We billed ourselves as a nonviolent cross-country meet — plus, the whistle never failed to work.

Great teachers plan when to use verbal cues and physical actions to regain everyone's focus before presenting essential parts of the lesson. When an elementary teacher raises their hand, everyone knows it is time to be quiet. There is no yelling or pleading, which no one wants to use or hear. When a teacher makes a unique move or shows something new, everyone wants to know what is happening. You may recall a lecturer holding up two fingers to signal that the class should pay attention because what they were about to say was probably going to be on the test.

> Great teachers plan when to use verbal cues and physical actions to regain everyone's focus before presenting essential parts of the lesson.

Absenteeism is a problem. Being in school does no good if students are mentally absent. Fight for their attention. Students need reasons to pay attention that overpower their misbelief that what is coming is not important.

Earlier in this book, I mentioned that, at times, it may be better to coach than to teach. What do great coaches do? Coaches spend time firing up their players so they can perform at their best. Do they do the same in their courses? If not, why not?

Foster strengthening mindsets. Coach-teachers choose their field of study because they think it is important. It is important to relay that mindset. If a coach-teacher wants the students to buy in, they must first demonstrate why they bought in to make the sale. It is not a matter of showing up and presenting. Students know when the person in front of them feels and believes in what they are teaching. Bring the energy.

MENTORING AND RE-MENTORING

Young teachers accelerate their growth, confidence, and mindsets through the benefits of mentoring. Tired teachers may reinvigorate themselves and reignite their fire through mentoring. All can benefit from rethinking and revisiting their approaches to presenting ideas to children. It is also good to re-mentor by consulting with or watching other great teachers at work.

THE FOUR DIVISIONS OF *SKILLS THROUGH PRESENTATIONS*

- **Division #1:** Each of the *Presentations for Students* can stand alone or be incorporated into multiple curriculum areas or programs to fit a school. The 120 presentations provide flexibility in the quantity and frequency of placement and delivery; e.g., if four teachers each do one a month for three years, the math is $4 \times 9 \times 3 = 108$. Certain teachers may do more than others. A school may use half of the presentations and still be very impactful. *Skills Through Presentations* complement other social-emotional programs. It has a high correlation to the heavily researched Boys Town *Social Skills* program.

- **Division #2:** *Skills for Parents* contains one hundred of the presentations in the master program's seven major categories in a reader-friendly format. Parents may read them on the school's website and then present or share the ideas with their child.

- **Division #3:** *Challenging College Workbook II* has dozens of planning activities to guide students who are considering post-secondary study. Some include exercises where parents compare their criteria for college selection with those of their student.

- **Division #4:** *Selling Your Curriculum* is recommended for teachers who want to increase student interest in their courses and content by "selling" their worth. Ready-to-use forms, information about where content is used in real-life careers, and sales pointers are available. Go to neilfeser.com for details on all divisions.

THINGS TO REMEMBER AND APPLY

○ It is difficult for one person to uplift a school, but not as hard to uplift the mindsets of a group who together can uplift the school.

○ Choose to fire up students or just be a filter. Make things happen or let them flow through you, not affecting you or anyone. If teachers see a lack of enthusiasm, insert a reason why the content is important. Do it early. Do it often. Anticipate it. Students want great reasons to take courses. Be bold. Be great.

○ Students know why they must be in school, but the same cannot be said for all courses. Teachers need to sell their fields, courses, and content. What is obvious to the teacher may not be to students.

○ Teachers in a department should create their own sales campaign and share or work on a campaign together. What works in one course can work in others to sell the field.

○ Salesmen teach customers *why* their product is great. Teachers must sell the worth of their content and concepts to students. Once everyone buys in, students' grades, teaching skills, and the school's overall success synergistically grow.

○ Changing low-end mindsets changes lives. It is essential that the disengaged be thrown lifelines. Show where course content can be used in society, employment, enjoyment, and helping others.

○ Young teachers accelerate growth and confidence via mentoring. Experienced teachers can too. It is never too late to reignite the fire.

CHAPTER 10

STOKE MOMENTUM OR PLAY CATCH-UP

Daring ideas are like chessmen moved forward;
they may be beaten, but they may start a winning game.
— GOETHE

It is the role of educators to clearly see what our students may not. The big picture is often in the details they may not know exist.

People have used many devices to see details and upgrade their vision. Long ago, our ancestors used polished crystals and clear glass containers filled with water to magnify small objects. Convex lenses made from glass have been used to read for more than a thousand years. Then, spectacles were developed, and in the late 1800s, the first contact lenses were made from blown glass. They were large, covering the eyeball, not just the cornea. Ouch. They were the early readers, not tri-level lenses.

We have come a long way, but the early inventors did not conceive of what was coming. We live in a world of electronic miracles, yet it is still hard for us to grasp or imagine what is coming.

SEEING THROUGH SMART CONTACT LENSES

Smart contact lenses exist in various stages of development. A commonly proposed design includes a lens with small screens positioned around the iris that can project information in front of the pupil. The apps on these screens will allow you to do many things, like access a compass to tell which direction you are looking, check your health, access the internet, etc. I am not including the latest research because, by the time you read this, it will be old news.

Batteries will be tiny and supported by another device worn on the body or in smartphones, etc. Like everything technology-related, this will introduce great opportunities as well as concerns. If students are allowed to wear smart contacts in class, it will be hard to keep them focused on the topic. A teacher in the future may interpret a smile to mean the student is tuned into the discussion when it is really a reaction to a basketball play or movie. Will a teacher be able to monitor what is on smart contacts in the same way they can check laptops from the front of the room through an immediate screen dump, or will someone come up with an app that polices contacts?

We do not think of smart-contact consciousness as muddy thinking, but if the student is supposed to be learning while watching sports, the mud will get deep fast. It will be a battle to sway eyes from social media or messaging apps. Will this be a means of sharing answers to a test? Do you hope you are retired before these technologies become available? Teachers need strong mindsets too. Relax. Have faith in Big Brother. Someone will come up with a way to jam the signal.

Technology will continue to advance, and educators will benefit from it and fight through it. This reinforces what was covered in Chapter 9. We must emphasize and sell the importance of field and course content to keep students focused on the subject matter and not the distractions of the world.

CATCHING UP TO THE PAST

With a few exceptions, the days of the *Little House on the Prairie* one-room schoolhouses are gone. In a way, one-room schools were better because while students worked on their homework, they also heard the instruction given to another group. They heard reviews of what they had learned in earlier grades or previews of what they would learn.

In the small town of Portsmouth, Iowa, the elementary school I attended could not afford a teacher for each grade, so two grades occupied the same room. I wonder if I retained the information better because of the preview and review process.

We modern educators might overconfidently think our students are superior until we look at the eighth-grade graduation examination used in Saline, Kansas, in 1895. The original copy of this examination is stored at the Smokey Valley Genealogical Society and Library, Inc.[12] A clearer copy of the full exam can be found on several websites. Here are the first and last challenges in the areas of the oral and written examination those "hicks" had to pass:

Examination Graduation Questions of Saline County, Kansas
April 13, 1895

Grammar (Time, one hour)
1. Give nine rules for the use of Capital Letters.
7. Write a composition of about 150 words and show therein that you understand the practical use of the rules of grammar.

Arithmetic (Time, 1+ hours)
1. Name and define the Fundamental Rules of Arithmetic.
10. Write a Bank Check, a Promissory Note, and a Receipt.

U.S. History (Time, 45 minutes)
1. Give the epochs into which U.S. History is divided.
8. Name events connected with the following dates: 1607, 1620, 1800, 1849, 1865.

Orthography (Time, one hour)
1. What is meant by the following: Alphabet, phonetic, orthography, etymology, syllabication?
10. Write 10 words frequently mispronounced and indicate pronunciation by use of diacritical marks and by syllabication.

Geography (Time, one hour)
1. What is climate? Upon what does climate depend?
10. Describe the movements of the earth. Give the inclination of the earth.

Physiology (Time, 45 minutes)
1. Where are the saliva, gastric juice, and bile secreted? What is the use of each in digestion?
10. Give some general directions that you think would be beneficial to preserve the human body in a state of health.

The above is less than 25 percent of the test. Most current eighth-grade students in the United States could not pass it. The truth is most high school seniors also could not pass this test. I will keep us adults out of it. You're welcome.

It appears we must pick up the pace to catch up with the past. Of course, it can be argued that we do not need to know the rules of arithmetic if calculators and artificial intelligence can do the work for us. That is partially true, yet we need to understand what the cohorts using artificial intelligence are doing. How do we organize, present, explain, fact-check, and justify anything without a good understanding of the techniques, procedures, theories, or methodologies involved in acquiring the facts and figures we are using? Without knowledge in our heads, how bad do we want to look if asked hard questions by the person paying our salaries?

The passing mark for the 1895 exam is not known. If those were the questions, it is safe to assume it was 70 percent, which was the standard for decades. What would those professional educators think of the 50 percent passing standard and the lowering of percentages to acquire an A, B, or C, as are the practices in some US public high schools? How does lowering those standards help? How does promoting that level of mindset elevate the mindsets of students who need to be able to show their value to employers?

There are pressures to get more students to graduate, but as I've stated in this book, are we going about it the right ways and through the right motivations? There are pressures to look good to parents and the public and to show grades that compete with other high schools. Who really believes that a 50 percent passing grade works? What does it cost, and what is lost? Ultimately, students, families, schools, and society lose. No aspiring educator went to college hoping they could work in a school that had 50 percent passing standards. That is deep mud.

How many employers are lining up to hire students who think it is acceptable to get 51 percent of a company's products made or orders filled correctly and still get paid? Students know that is not going to happen in any job. Why are they led to believe it is acceptable in school?

When students say the two worlds are not the same because work is real and school is not, counter that argument by explaining school is closer to the world of better-paying jobs. Repetitive jobs that require no analysis or school-related skills do not pay well and will be gradually phased out by machines run by artificial intelligence.

People who pick up garbage are paid well and should be. How long before the only person picking it up is the one driving the truck while robots pick up the containers and leave the things the driver looking at screens in the cab says to leave? How long before the truck has no driver at all, and a person sitting in a distant room monitors several trucks? How long before there is no person sitting in the room to monitor anything?

There must be an intentional effort to get the seriousness of preparing for future work opportunities across to those who think they can drop out or opt out and be prepared for a very different future. We must energize the fire in students, or they will spend most of their lives trying to catch up financially, which directly or indirectly affects so much of our lives.

GET UP, MAKE UP, MOVE UP, STAY UP

The decision to do what it takes to graduate is simple, but it takes more than a decision. It takes work to get caught up if behind, to make up work that was thought to be un-important, to move up so that skills are gained to make the student not just a future employee, but someone worthy of advancing to higher and better-paying jobs, and to stay up with the needs of future schooling and work.

Every school should set the expectation that all students are going to graduate from programs that are worthy of emulation, not substandard admission of failure to meet worthy standards. A mind set on not graduating is a "mudset." Refuse to lose students.

Once everyone buys into the graduation mindset, the next mindset that needs to be adopted is that everyone is going to go on to higher education. This could be as an apprentice for months or years or a successful career in college.

Put the feet of students to the fire of reality before they are out of your door. Do not wait for them to leave. Throw their attitude and poor vision of the future up against the wall and make them face reality before they are gone. To help you do this, review, use, and download the presentation *Dropouts Drop Dollars*.

A great effort must be made to enrich courses with reasons to finish them. Great courses entice students to stay and desire growth that allows them to graduate and avoid low-end, low-paying jobs for years if not decades. The stress of working multiple, low-paying jobs that have poor work hours affects workers and their families. The truth is not complicated. The reality of not being prepared for the real world is.

WRITE AND LIVE YOUR LETTER OF RECOMMENDATION

In their sophomore year or early in their junior year, I had students write a letter of recommendation for themselves. They had to show what they were accomplishing or face a nearly blank page. If they were going to college, there was still time to build up their resume.

Some experts have people write their obituaries. That was my original idea, but students do not think that far. Do educators? I am more concerned with what educators are doing and will do in the next few years. Every educator should write their own letter of recommendation every five years. Ask these questions and more about your educational work history with emphasis on what is currently in motion and offer specific examples:

- What have you demonstrated through your actions to be important?
- What ideals did you set, meet, and revise?
- Where has your time been invested?
- Identify opportunities you maximized.
- Should your results be posted, remembered, emulated, or corrected?
- How was learning modeled?
- When was learning and mindset ever remodeled? For what reason(s)?
- When were students and colleagues inspired, elevated, or bored by your work? Are you brave enough to own up to this? It can help if you relate why and how you attacked that instance for students.

- How many students and colleagues would ask for more from you?
- How did your personal goals, efforts, and results make a difference?
- What are your strong points, and how are you elevating them?
- How do you best like to serve?
- What makes you unique and a valuable team member?

Educators are the front line. Educators step up, step to the side, or stand in place. The latter two, unfortunately, get in the way of growth. The last is an option for adults in many jobs, but not one for an educator. Educators continually build up students or are dead weight on the school, students, and colleagues. They are in seriously deep mud. The world moves on with or without us, but the educational life of students withers and muddies without our best efforts.

The lives of students and their descendants for generations are not pawns in a game. What do students' eyes say about what is being done now to help their lives? The lives behind those eyes are instrumental in creating our collective future.

The thousands of lives educators inspire will do more for the world than any one person can. And often, it is not the smartest in the classroom or the richest or the most favored who is the most successful. We cannot know which student will rise to the top, so we raise all boats so they can set themselves free.

It may not be one of the students who a current teacher inspires that makes the biggest difference in the world. It might be the grandchild of someone we help that transforms our reality. We do not just educate the students in front of us. We educate generations.

Educators continuously raise their level of play and that of students, future families, citizens, and leaders, which is essential to a better world. Will they feel inspired to step up or lie down? Mindsets matter.

> It may not be one of the students who a current teacher inspires that makes the biggest difference in the world. It might be the grandchild of someone we help that transforms our reality.

Educators must relish the opportunity to inspire, execute, and accomplish. The work is never done, and neither are we. Play on.

GENERATIONS OF IMPACT

Skills Through Presentations is designed to be effective and impactful for decades. This lowers its per-pupil cost, which is found at neilfeser.com. Be a developer of vibrant mindsets free of mud and growing in confidence.

As suggested earlier, will you consider helping students in schools you will never visit or know about? If you learned from this book, please give it to a colleague and buy the inexpensive eBook on Amazon so you can write a brief review there about how it helped you.

Your effort may move others to learn from this book and help students who will never know your name but who will gain from your small kindness because you moved someone to help them.

Be part of a growing mindset.

Be part of the synergy.

THINGS TO REMEMBER AND APPLY

o Technology continues to advance, and educators will benefit from it and fight through it. What are the best questions we should be asking to prepare for another revolution in education when information is available in formats we have not considered?

o School is closer to the real world of good-paying jobs. We must energize the fire in students to act for their own benefit, or they will spend their lives trying to catch up financially.

o Every school should achieve the expectation that all students are going to graduate from programs that are worthy of emulation. Once everyone buys into the graduation mindset, the next mindset to adopt is that everyone goes on to higher education, be that as an apprentice or through college.

o The truth of preparing for the future is not complicated. The reality of not being prepared for the real world is. Foster a growth mindset. How does your letter of recommendation for yourself read? You have time to improve. Live up to your greatness. It believes in you.

o Are advantages gained by lowering learning standards and the grades required to reach them? Who is served? Who is cheated? Educators are the front line. They step up, to the side, or stand in place. The latter two can impede growth and are not options for educators.

o Often, it is not the smartest in the classroom or the richest or the most favored who is the most successful. We raise everyone so they can set themselves free.

ENDNOTES

1 "Population of the United States in 1960: Introduction." United States Census Bureau. Accessed December 17, 2024. https://www2.census.gov/library/publications/decennial/1860/population/1860a-02.pdf.

2 "Global Slavery Index." Walk Free. Accessed August 12, 2024. https://www.walkfree.org/global-slavery-index/.

3 Davis, John. "Border Crisis: CBP Fights Child Exploitation." U.S. Customs and Border Protection, January 4, 2022. https://www.cbp.gov/frontline/border-crisis-cbp-fights-child-exploitation.

4 "Global Slavery Index." Walk Free. Accessed August 12, 2024. https://www.walkfree.org/global-slavery-index/.

5 Exact numbers are not available. These statistics are estimates and based on my decades of professional experience in the education system.

6 "Suicide Data and Statistics." Centers for Disease Control and Prevention, October 29, 2024. https://www.cdc.gov/suicide/facts/data.html.

7 "Substance Use in Adolescence." HHS Office of Population Affairs, n.d. https://opa.hhs.gov/adolescent-health/substance-use-adolescence#:~:text=Tobacco%20use%20remains%20the.

8 Zablotsky, Benjamin Ph.D., Ng, Amanda E., Ph.D., M.P.H., Black, Lindsey I., M.P.H., Bose, Jonaki, Ph.D.,

Jones, Jessica R., Ph.D., M.P.H., Maitland, Aaron K., Ph.D., Blumberg, Stephen J., Ph.D. "Perceived Social and Emotional Support Among Teenagers: United States, July 2021–December 2022." Centers for Disease Control and Prevention, July 16, 2024. https://www.cdc.gov/nchs/data/nhsr/nhsr206.pdf.

9   "High School Graduation Rates." National Center for Education Statistics, May 2024. https://nces.ed.gov/programs/coe/indicator/coi/high-school-graduation-rates.

10 "Fast Facts: Dropout Rates." National Center for Education Statistics, n.d. https://nces.ed.gov/fastfacts/display.asp?id=16#:~:text=The%20status%dropout%20rate%20for%2016-%20to%2024-year-olds,lowest%20Gr%20those%20who%20were%20Asian%20%281.9%20percent%.

11 *Occupational Outlook Handbook,* U.S. Bureau of Labor Statistics, (December 20, 2024), Home : Occupational Outlook Handbook: : U.S. Bureau of Labor Statistics https://www.bls.gov/ooh/.

12 Smoky Valley Genealogical Society & Library, Inc. "1895 8th Grade Exam." Smoky Valley Genealogical Society & Library, Inc., 2022. https://www.splks.org/1895-8th-grade-exam.html.

ABOUT THE AUTHOR

Neil Feser, author of *Challenging College, Challenging College Workbook, The Book of Yo*, and the *Skills Through Presentations* program, is a successful keynote speaker and presenter at conventions, workshops, schools, and college campuses and has worked as a school counselor, teacher, and college administrator. He began his writing career working for professional comedians and is published in multiple genres, journals, newsletters, and media.

For many years, Feser had a private counseling and therapy practice. His popular stress-reduction workshops helped teachers, parents, teams, and students.

His wide-ranging career includes directing plays, improvisational theatre, consulting, and teaching hypnosis at the American College of Hypnotherapy. Long before the US government gave it credence, he assisted Dr. Jack Kasher, a physics professor at the University of Nebraska Omaha, in conducting research on UFOs and UAPs (unidentified aerial phenomenon) and "alien" abductions. We'll skip the part when he walked on burning coals.

CONTACT

Go to neilfeser.com for current contact information.

www.ingramcontent.com/pod-product-compliance
Lightning Source LLC
Chambersburg PA
CBHW071144120626
46546CB00006B/2124